MAGIC TREE HOUSE®

Games and Puzzles from the Tree House

by Mary Pope Osborne
and Natalie Pope Boyce

illustrated by Sal Murdocca

A STEPPING STONE BOOK™

Random House 🏠 New York

Visit us on the Web!
www.magictreehouse.com
www.randomhouse.com/kids

Educators and librarians, for a variety of teaching tools,
visit us at www.randomhouse.com/teachers

ISBN 978-0-375-86216-8

Printed in the United States of America
10 9 8 7 6 5 4 3 2 1

Dinosaurs Before Dark

Maze

Help Jack get back to the tree house without running into the Tyrannosaurus rex.

Finish

Start

1

Answer key on page 225.

Connect-the-Dots

Start at 1, and connect the dots to see the mother of these dinosaur babies.

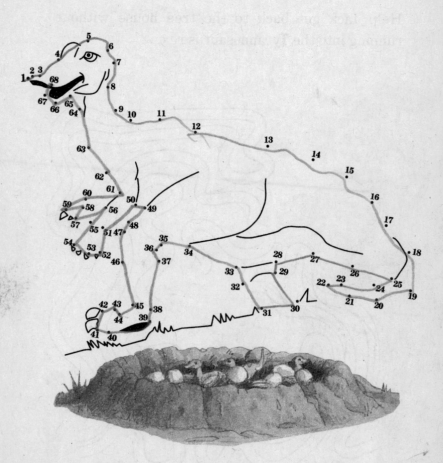

Answer key on page 225.

Illustrate It!

Draw the dinosaur that Jack is looking at.

Code Breaker

Use the reverse alphabet code (A = Z, B = Y, C = X, and so on) to help Jack and Annie figure out how they can know when the tree house is taking them somewhere new.

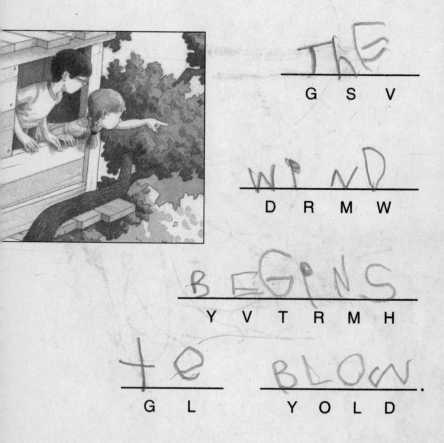

THE
G S V

WIND
D R M W

BEGINS
Y V T R M H

TO   BLOW.
G   L   Y O L D

Answer key on page 225.

Triangle Mystery

Color in each three-sided shape to reveal a friendly dinosaur.

Answer key on page 225.

The Knight at Dawn

Word Search

Find and circle the words below. Words can go horizontally, vertically, or diagonally.

**Armor · Bow · Castle · Court
Dungeon · Feast · Moat · Sword**

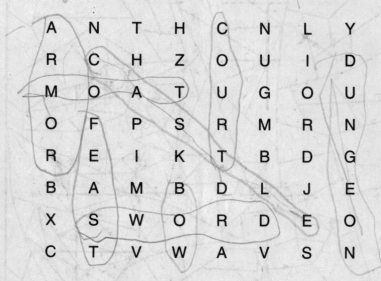

A	N	T	H	C	N	L	Y
R	C	H	Z	O	U	I	D
M	O	A	T	U	G	O	U
O	F	P	S	R	M	R	N
R	E	I	K	T	B	D	G
B	A	M	B	D	L	J	E
X	S	W	O	R	D	E	O
C	T	V	W	A	V	S	N

6

Tic-Tac-Toe

Find a friend, sibling, or parent and challenge him or her to a tic-tac-toe duel. Choose whether you want to be an X or an O. Take turns, and mark your letter in one of the nine tic-tac-toe squares. If you get three of your marks in a row horizontally, vertically, or diagonally, you win!

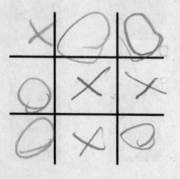
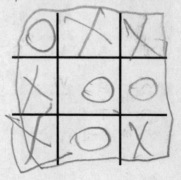

Book Battle

Find a friend, sibling, or parent and challenge him or her to a battle for books. Take turns drawing lines connecting the books, one line at a time, to make a square. Lines can go horizontally or vertically, but not diagonally. The player who completes a square gets to put his or her initial inside it and take another turn. The player with more squares wins. Jack has made the first move here.

Matching

Jack and Annie learn that the armor knights wore was really heavy. The helmet alone could weigh up to forty pounds! Draw lines connecting the coats of arms that are the same.

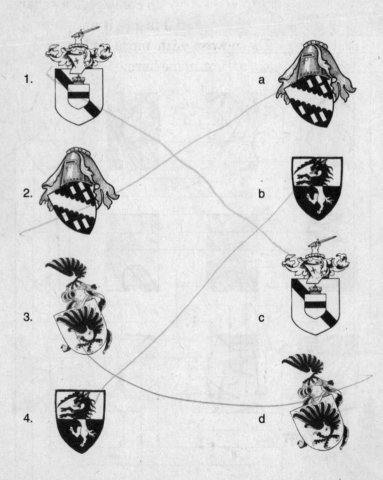

Answer key on page 225.

Maze

Help Jack and Annie find their way through the secret tunnels of the castle to the outside.

FINISH

START

Answer key on page 226.

Mummies in the Morning

Spot the Differences

Look at the picture on the left. Then look at the picture on the right and circle the five differences.

Answer key on page 226.

Hieroglyphic Alphabet

The ancient Egyptians wrote using pictures called hieroglyphs (say HY-ro-GLIFS). Use the hieroglyphic alphabet below to draw your name on the line.

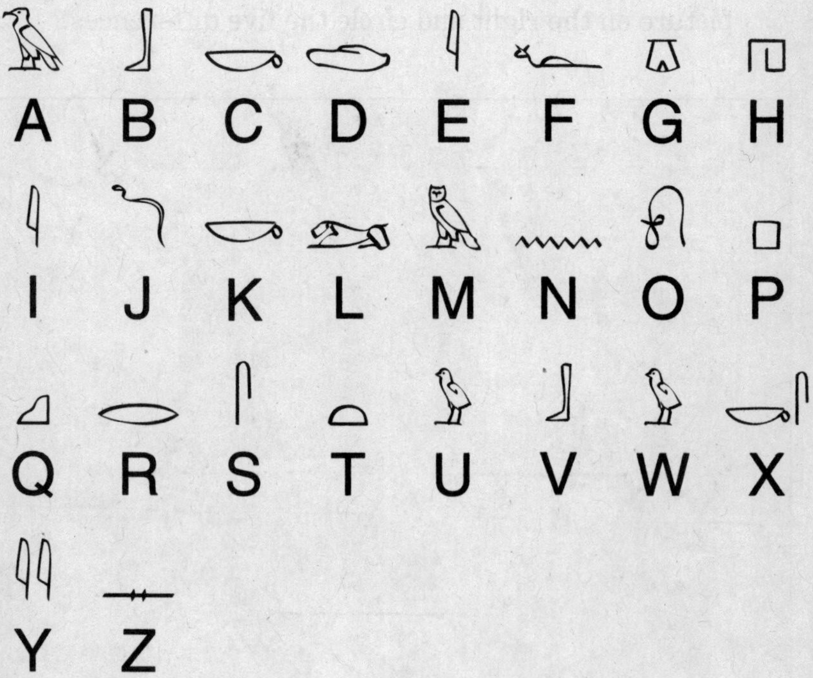

A B C D E F G H

I J K L M N O P

Q R S T U V W X

Y Z

Code Breaker

Use the hieroglyphic alphabet from page twelve to break the code and get an important message from the mysterious M. The slash means there is a space between words. Be careful! Some hieroglyphs can be used for two different letters, so this code is trickier than it looks.

follow   the

cat

to   SAFiTY

Mummy Scramble

Jack and Annie were surprised to learn that ancient Egyptians dried out bodies with salt, covered them with oil, and wrapped them tightly in bandages to make mummies. Unscramble the words below. Then use the letters in the circles to find out why you can trust mummies with your secrets.

dmaripy   P Y R A M I D

erdest   ☐ ☐ ☐ ☐ ◯ ☐

wmoe   ☐ ☐ ☐ ◯

lfraenu   ☐ ☐ ☐ ☐ ☐ ◯ ☐

tshog   ☐ ☐ ☐ ◯ ☐

They'll keep your secrets under ◯ ◯ ◯ ◯ ◯ !

14

Crossword Puzzle

Use the clues for Across and Down to fill in the puzzle spaces.

Across

3. Beasts of burden used in processions
5. Ancient Egyptian writing
6. False passages were built to stop these
7. A dried, preserved body

Down

1. Coffin of a royal person
2. Gold stick carried by kings and queens
4. Sometimes called a House of the Dead

7. MUMMY

Answer key on page 226.

Pirates Past Noon

Illustrate It!

Below is the pirate flag called the Jolly Roger. Draw your own pirate flag beneath it.

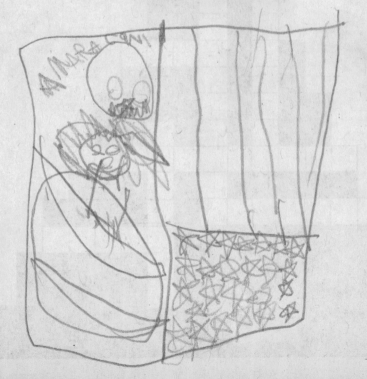

Maze

Help Jack and Annie lead Cap'n Bones to the place where Captain Kidd's treasure is buried. X marks the spot!

START

FINISH

17

Answer key on page 226.

Word Search

Find and circle the words below. Words can go horizontally, vertically, or diagonally.

**Chest · Dig · Gold · Island · Map
Parrot · Pirates · Treasure**

N G K C E S T E
C H E S T X R P
P D I G I U A I
A I G V S M E R
R M I A L N G A
R P E R A S O T
O R Q P N V L E
T B X A D Y D S

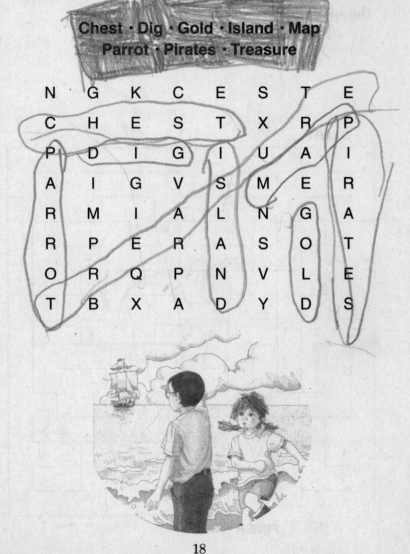

Answer key on page 227.

Compass Game

Use the compass to follow the directions and get Jack and Annie's ship to the X that marks the real hidden treasure.

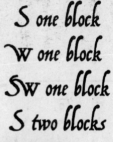

S one block

W one block

Sw one block

S two blocks

START

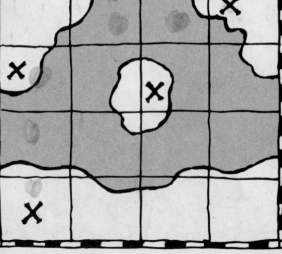

19

Answer key on page 227.

Code Breaker

Use the reverse alphabet code (A = Z, B = Y, C = X, and so on) to help Jack and Annie figure out how Cap'n Bones was able to buy his ship.

_____ _____
   G S V   H S R K

_____ _____ _____.
  D Z H   L M   H Z R O

20

Answer key on page 227.

Night of the Ninjas

Ninja Note

Imagine that you are a ninja. You've just received an important message, but it's in code! Cross out any letters in the word "sword" to read the note.

Answer key on page 227.

Illustrate It!

Draw your own ninja below. Make sure you give your ninja a tool for battling enemies and a tool for climbing trees. What else might your ninja need?

Follow Nature

The way of the ninja taught Jack and Annie to learn from nature. Match each animal below with a skill that a ninja might learn from it.

1. Cheetah   b   a. Blend in with your surroundings.

2. Mouse   e   b. Run swiftly.

3. Kangaroo   c   c. Jump far.

4. Raccoon   f   d. Climb walls.

5. Chameleon   a   e. Move quietly.

6. Spider   d   f. See well in the dark.

Answer key on page 227.

Ninja vs. Samurai

Find a friend, sibling, or parent and challenge him or her to a battle. Take turns drawing lines connecting the ninja stars, one line at a time, to make a square. Lines can go horizontally or vertically, but not diagonally. The player who completes a square gets to put his or her initial inside it and take another turn. The player with more squares wins. Jack has made the first move here.

Race to the Tree House

Jack, Annie, and Peanut are in a hurry to get back to the magic tree house. But they all have a different idea of how to get there. Find out whose way will get them back safely!

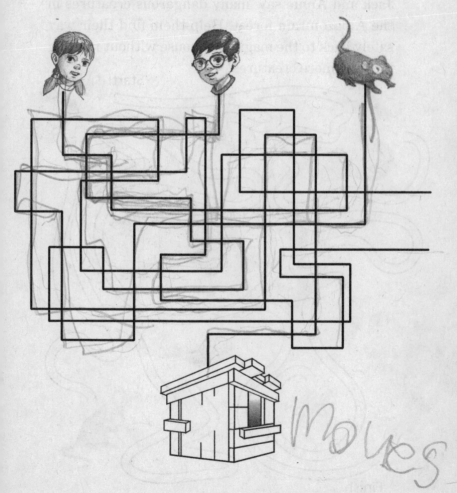

Answer key on page 227.

Afternoon on the Amazon

Maze

Jack and Annie saw many dangerous creatures in
the Amazon rain forest. Help them find their way
safely back to the magic tree house without running
into any more creatures!

Start

Finish

26

Answer key on page 227.

Triangle Mystery

Many animals of the rain forest are camouflaged. That makes them difficult to see. Color in each three-sided shape to reveal a hidden animal.

ALAGATR

27

Answer key on page 228.

Matching

Draw lines connecting each animal with the part of the Amazon rain forest where you would be most likely to find that animal.

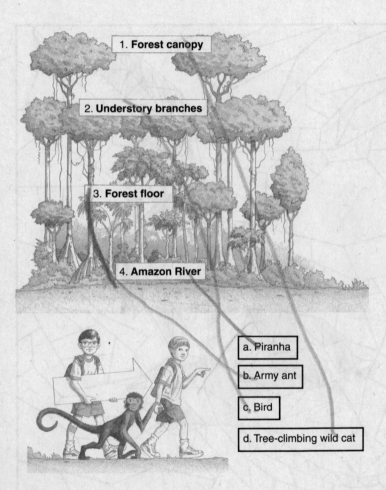

1. **Forest canopy**

2. **Understory branches**

3. **Forest floor**

4. **Amazon River**

a. Piranha

b. Army ant

c. Bird

d. Tree-climbing wild cat

Answer key on page 228.

Illustrate It!

Annie has found an animal on the forest floor! Using your knowledge of what animals live in the rain forest, draw what you think she found in the space provided.

Habitat Match

Jack and Annie see so many different things on their travels, they sometimes have trouble remembering where they saw what! Circle the animals below that belong in the Amazon rain forest. Put an X through any animal that doesn't belong.

Jaguar   Monkey

Penguin   Camel

Vampire bat Butterfly

Crocodile   Army ant

Kangaroo   Polar bear

Answer key on page 228.

Sunset of the Sabertooth

Caveman Creations

Cro-Magnons used animals, plants, and stones to make many different objects. Help Jack and Annie match each material on the left with the object that Cro-Magnons could make with it.

1. reindeer skins _____ a. axes and knives

2. plant fibers _____ b. lamps

3. stones _____ c. clothing

4. mammoth bones _____ d. rope

5. animal fat and moss _____ e. flutes

Answer key on page 228.

Illustrate It!

Make your own painting of Ice Age beasts based on Jack and Annie's descriptions of Cro-Magnon cave paintings. Be sure to use authentic colors, such as red, black, and yellow.

Musical Notes

Jack used a flute made of mammoth bone to calm a sabertooth tiger. There is a hidden message in the music he played. Can you decode it? A vertical line means a space between words.

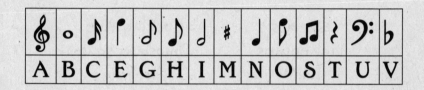

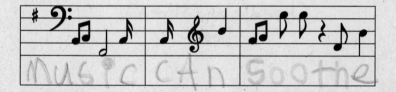

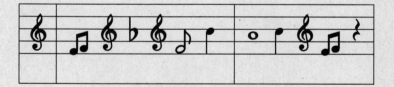

Answer key on page 228.

Cro-Magnon Wish List

Jack and Annie have been inside the cave of a Cro-Magnon family. But they are having a hard time remembering what items Cro-Magnons might have in their homes. Read the list below and cross out anything you definitely wouldn't find in the Ice Age.

Spears   Cooking fire

Lightbulbs   Dinosaur soup

Paint   Clothing

Musical instruments

Eyeglasses

Needle and thread

Books

Answer key on page 228.

Rebus Fun

Use the combinations of pictures and letters to spell out the names of animals that lived during the Ice Age.

Answer key on page 228.

Midnight on the Moon

I Spy on the Moon

Go outside, or look out the window if you're in a car. Try to spot all the objects on the list below. As you spot them, say whether you could find that thing on the moon.

Tree   Cloud

Bird   Rock

Flag   Footprint

Water

Answer key on page 228.

Maze

Help Jack and Annie drive their moon buggy to the American flag.

FINISH

START

Answer key on page 228.

Word Search

Find and circle the words below. Words can go horizontally, vertically, or diagonally. The letters you don't circle will spell out a hidden message!

Moon · Planet · Space · Stars · Sun

S	S	T	A	R	S
M	P	W	E	S	C
O	O	A	M	U	E
O	I	N	C	N	P
N	E	A	C	E	E
P	L	A	N	E	T

Answer key on page 229.

Connect-the-Stars

Start at 1, and connect the stars to create a brand-new constellation. Hint: It's an animal!

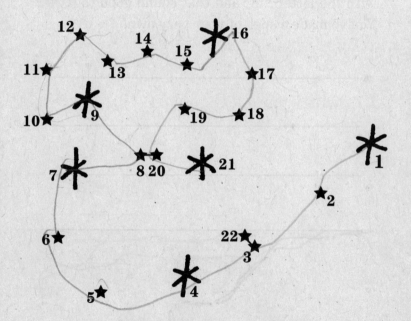

Answer key on page 229.

Break the Spell!

Jack and Annie collected four things that start with the letter "m": moonstone, mango, mammoth bone, and mouse. Saying all four words together created a spell to help Morgan. But what if they had found other objects instead?

Come up with four objects or animals that start with the letter "m" and that sound good together. You've made a spell of your very own!

_____

_____

_____

_____

Dolphins at Daybreak

Crossword Puzzle

Use the clues for Across and Down to fill in the puzzle spaces.

ACROSS

2. Answer to the riddle
4. Jack rode to safety on
6. Three feet wide and weighs up to 200 lbs. (2 words)
7. These let water in to fill the mini-sub
8. Main enemy of the octopus

DOWN

1. Saved Jack and Annie
3. Swim like this if you see a shark
5. Tiny sea animals

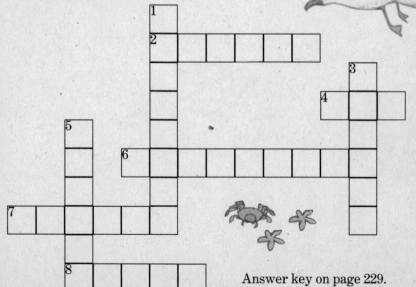

Answer key on page 229.

Illustrate It!

Scientists who study the ocean are called oceanographers. Jack and Annie used the oceanographers' mini-sub to see the strange and beautiful sea life on a coral reef. Draw what Jack and Annie see out of the mini-sub's window.

Fishing for Similarities

Jack's research book says, "Nearly 5,000 different species of fish live around coral reefs in the Indian and Pacific Oceans." Look at the fish below. Circle the two fish that are exactly the same.

Answer key on page 229.

Maze

Computers are used to guide mini-subs through the ocean, but this mini-sub's computer is broken! Help Jack and Annie guide the mini-sub out of the coral reef to safety.

Finish

Start

Answer key on page 229.

Say Again?

Jack and Annie learn that even though dolphins and sharks live in the same waters, they are very different animals. Draw speech bubbles and write in what you think a dolphin and a shark might say to one another.

Ghost Town at Sundown

Q & A Mix-up

See if you can find the questions to the answers Jack and Annie have discovered about ghost towns. Don't forget to start each one with *Who* or *What*.

An early version of this instrument played automatically when someone pumped its floor pedals.

_____

Descendants of runaway Spanish horses, these wild animals wandered in herds in the Old West.

_____

These mean-spirited men stole mustangs from herders.

_____

46

Answer key on page 229.

Ghost Town Scramble

Jack and Annie chase down horse thieves with a cowboy named Slim. Unscramble the words below. Then use the letters in the circles to learn the first rule on how to treat a horse.

gtamsun ☐ ☐ ☐ ◯ ☐ ☐ ☐

rhsoe ◯ ☐ ☐ ◯ ☐

dldsae ☐ ◯ ◯ ☐ ☐ ☐

efofce ☐ ◯ ☐ ◯ ☐ ☐

nycaon ☐ ☐ ◯ ☐ ☐ ☐

Use a ◯◯◯◯ ◯◯◯◯.

47

Answer key on page 229.

Mustang Mamas

Jack and Annie learn that mustangs live together in families and that the bond between a mare and her young is very strong. Follow the path to find out which mare is the mother of this colt.

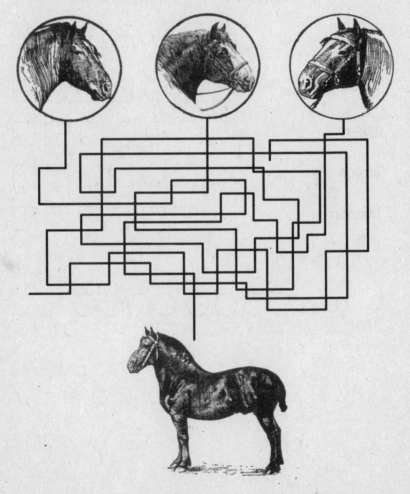

Answer key on page 230.

Musical Notes

Player pianos were popular in the Wild West. Lonesome Luke left a message for Jack, Annie, and you in this piece of sheet music. A vertical line means a space between words.

| A | B | C | D | E | H | I | N | O | R | S | T | U | Y |

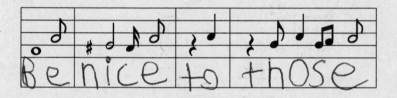

Be nice to those

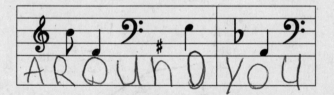

AROUND you

Connect-the-Dots

Start at 1, and connect the dots to see what bothers Jack throughout *Ghost Town at Sundown*.

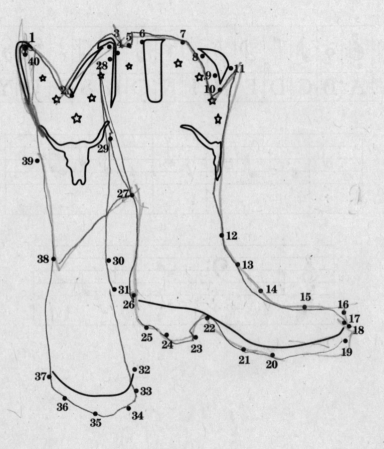

Answer key on page 230.

Lions at Lunchtime

Morgan's Message

Unscramble the letters below and reorder them in the spaces provided to see Morgan's special message to Jack, Annie, and you, too!

E B   A B R E V

E B   E I W S

E B   R C E A F L U

BE Brave.

BE wise.

BE CAREFUE.

Answer key on page 230.

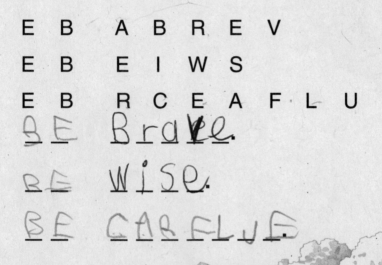

Illustrate It!

Jack and Annie see a lot of cool animals on the African plains. Draw your favorite African animal below.

Zebra of a Different Stripe

Every zebra has its own unique pattern of stripes, sort of the way you have your own special fingerprints. The zebras below are all the same—except for one! Circle the zebra that is different.

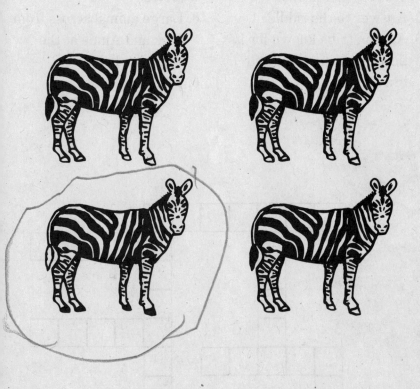

Answer key on page 230.

Crossword Puzzle

Use the clues for Across and Down to fill in the puzzle spaces.

ACROSS
1. Strange animal spotted in Frog Creek, Pennsylvania
4. These frighten Jack
5. Answer to the riddle
6. African tribe known for its fierce fighting skills and bravery

DOWN
2. These chew down the grass before the wildebeests arrive
3. Large animal across from Jack and Annie at the watering hole
6. Trapped Annie

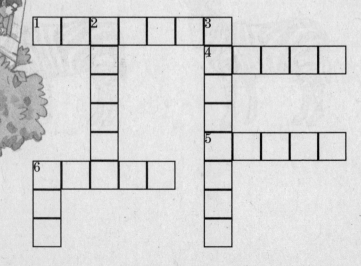

54

Answer key on page 230.

Rebus Fun

Use the combinations of pictures and letters to spell out the names of important animals and characters from *Lions at Lunchtime*.

L + [eye] + [switch ON/OFF]

_L_ion_____

[apron] + O + [pot] + A + [rat]

hipopotAmous_____

M + [oar] + G + & - D

[leg] - G F + [hay]

Morgan Lee fay_____

[calendar MONDAY 5] - DAY + [keys]

_____

[ant] - T + [foot]

_____

Answer key on page 231.

Polar Bears Past Bedtime

Polar Bear Scramble

Help Jack and Annie answer the questions below.
Then unscramble the letters in the circles to find out
the place that Jack and Annie love best.

1. What is the answer to the riddle?

⬭ ▢ ▢ ▢

2. Who helps Jack and Annie?

▢ ▢ ▢ ▢ ⬭ ▢ ▢ ▢ ▢ ▢

3. How do Arctic people get around?

▢ ▢ ▢ ▢ ▢ ⬭ ▢

4. What are caused by electrically charged particles from
the sun striking atoms and molecules in the earth's
atmosphere?

▢ ⬭ ▢ ▢ ▢ ▢ ▢ ▢
▢ ▢ ▢ ▢ ▢ ▢

⬭ ⬭ ⬭ ⬭

Answer key on page 231.

Word Search

Find and circle the words below. Words can go horizontally, vertically, or diagonally.

**Arctic · Bear · Cub · Freezing · Hunter
Husky · Igloo · Tundra**

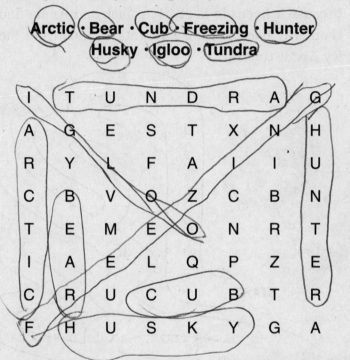

```
I   T   U   N   D   R   A   G
A   G   E   S   T   X   N   H
R   Y   L   F   A   I   I   U
C   B   V   O   Z   C   B   N
T   E   M   E   O   N   R   T
I   A   E   L   Q   P   Z   E
C   R   U   C   U   B   T   R
F   H   U   S   K   Y   G   A
```

Answer key on page 231.

Maze

Jack and Annie learn that native Arctic people built igloos with blocks of snow. Dry snow is best because it keeps in heat. Help Jack and Annie find their way back to the seal hunter's igloo from the icy Arctic tundra.

START

FINISH

Answer key on page 231.

Who Turned On the Lights?

Was it the polar bear spirit or charged particles from the sun striking atoms and molecules in the earth's atmosphere that filled the Arctic sky with swirls of red, green, and purple light? Using crayons, colored pencils, or markers, bring the northern lights to the blank skies shown below.

Connect-the-Dots

Jack and Annie have succeeded in their quest. They are now Master Librarians! Start at 1, and connect the dots to reveal one of their friends.

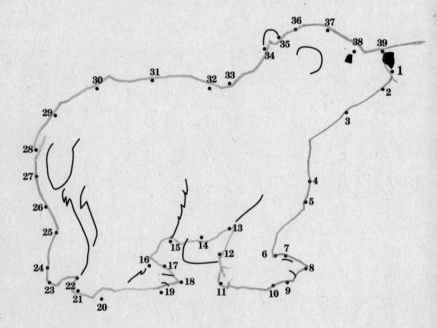

Answer key on page 231.

Vacation Under the Volcano Matching

Jack and Annie are saved by Hercules, hero to the Greeks and Romans and son of the Roman god Jupiter. See if you can match the Roman gods listed below with their Greek equivalents. Don't be surprised if many of these names are familiar!

**Ceres • Cupid • Diana • Jupiter • Mars
Mercury • Minerva • Neptune • Saturn • Venus**

Greek gods	Role	Roman gods
1. Zeus	King of the gods	_____
2. Poseidon	God of the sea	_____
3. Athena	Goddess of wisdom	_____
4. Aphrodite	Goddess of love	_____
5. Ares	God of war	_____
6. Eros	God of love	_____
7. Hermes	Messenger of the gods	_____
8. Artemis	Goddess of the moon	_____
9. Cronus	God of time	_____
10. Demeter	Goddess of harvest	_____

Answer key on page 231.

Vocabulary Challenge

Latin was the official language of the Roman Empire. Write an English word that comes from the following Latin roots. The first one is done for you.

Latin Root	English Meaning	English Word
Act	Act, Do	Activity
Flect	Flex, Bend	Flexible
Leg	Read, Choose	_____
Ped	Foot	_____
Pend	Hang	_____
Port	Carry	_____
Scrib	Write	_____
Sent	Feel	_____
Spect	Look	_____
Vict	Conquer	_____
Voc	Call	_____

Answer key on page 231.

Roman Crisscross

Can you fit all eight of the following words into the puzzle below without any clues? If there are any words or names you don't know, look them up and expand your vocabulary!

Gladiator • Hercules • Jupiter • Papyrus • Pompeii Soothsayer • Sundial • Vesuvius

Answer key on page 231.

Sightseeing

Jack and Annie looked all over the ancient Roman town of Pompeii for a library. Along the way, they saw many other places and learned a bit about life in ancient Rome. Can you match each place with what it was used for?

1. **Forum** ____ a. Washing and swimming

2. **Amphitheater** ____ b. Worshipping gods and goddesses

3. **Villa** ____ c. Watching gladiators fight

4. **Public baths** ____ d. Buying and selling goods

5. **Temple** ____ e. Private living

Answer key on page 232.

Worth Quoting

The letters below are scrambled, but they are in the correct columns. Figure out where to place each letter to write out a famous saying that means "Follow the rules and customs of the place you are visiting."

W	D	R	N	A	S	N	T	R	D	O	E
	H	E	O	M	A	N	S	H	O	M	
		O		I					E		
				■		■					
■			■			■			■	■	■
■	■					■					

Answer key on page 232.

Day of the Dragon King

Illustrate It!

When the Chinese discovered how to make silk, they were able to make beautiful and colorful clothing. Below, design a new robe for the emperor. What colors would you use? Would you include dragons or horses, or simply lines and shapes?

Maze

Jack and Annie are lost in the tomb of the Dragon King! Help them find their way out.

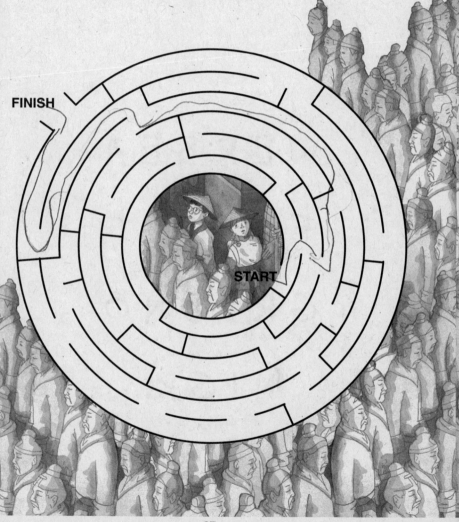

FINISH

START

Answer key on page 232.

Great Wall Scramble

A Chinese scholar has left a coded message for Jack and Annie on the Great Wall of China. Can you unscramble the message?

WERBEA
FO/HET
GRADNO
NIGK.

Answer key on page 232.

Silk Tangle

The silk weaver has left trails of thread behind her, but two of the trails are meant to confuse the Dragon King. Help Jack and Annie find the thread that will lead them to their new friend!

Answer key on page 232.

Code Breaker

Crickets were kept as pets long ago in China because of the soothing sounds they make. Imagine that your pet cricket can "talk" to you using Morse code, which is an alphabet of simple sounds. Use the key below to decipher what the cricket might say!

Morse Code Alphabet Key

A ._		N _.
B _...		O ___
C _._.		P .__.
D _..		Q __._
E .		R ._.
F .._.		S ...
G __.		T _
H		U .._
I ..		V ..._
J .___		W .__
K _._		X _.._
L ._..		Y _.__
M __		Z __..

.__. ._.. . ._ ... .
P L E A S E

.._. . . _.. __ .
F E E D M E

_ . ._ _._. . ._ ..._ . ...
T E A C E A V E S

Answer key on page 232.

Viking Ships at Sunrise

Judge a Book by Its Cover

Help Brother Michael complete the cover of his handwritten book. It's called *Serpens Magna*. Write the title in your fanciest letters on the line provided. Then decorate the cover with a border, gleaming jewel shapes, and bright colors.

Vocabulary Challenge

Test your knowledge by answering the questions below. Then read the letters in the circles to learn the Latin word for "great."

Who lives in monasteries?

(m) O n K S

What part of a ship catches wind?

S (a) i l

What's another term for the Middle Ages?

D a r k a (g) e S

What's another word for a large snake?

S e r p (e) (n) t

What do you use to move a boat when there's no wind?

O (a) r s

Bonus question: Now that you know the Latin word for "great," can you translate the title of the book on page 71?

_____ magna _____

Answer key on page 232.

Writers Across the Ages

Jack and Annie have learned about the many different ways stories have been written throughout history. See if you can match each writer with the description of how he or she works.

a. A monk in the Dark Ages

b. A Chinese scholar in the time of the Dragon King

c. A Roman writer of myths

1. I have to write everything by hand. Instead of a pen, I use a goose feather as a quill, and instead of paper, I use sheepskin. My paints are made of earth and plants. When I am finished, I have created a colorful book. _____

2. I write using a small reed as a pen. I dip the pen in ink that is made partly from octopus ink. When I am finished, I have created a "book" that is really a scroll of papyrus paper. _____

3. I do not use letters when I write. My language is made up of over 50,000 different characters. When I am finished, I have created a "book" made of many bamboo strips tied in a bundle. _____

Bonus question: Can you guess what tool Mary Pope Osborne uses to write the Magic Tree House books?

_____

Answer key on page 232.

Viking Mix-up

Something is wrong with the picture below. Can you figure out what?

Answer key on page 233.

Illustrate It!

Imagine that you've been asked to design a new Viking ship. Draw your design in the space below. Don't forget to give the prow a scary serpent head. You also might want to include a sail, oars, and a rope for docking.

Hour of the Olympics

Connect-the-Dots

Start at 1, and connect the dots to see the mythical creature that is also a constellation.

Answer key on page 233.

Maze

How quickly can you run the footrace called the Stade? It was the only event in the first Olympic games.

Answer key on page 233.

Vocabulary Challenge

Many English words come from the Greek language. Can you match the English word to its Greek meaning?

1. **Philosophy** ____   a. Study of life

2. **Anonymous** ____   b. Star arrangement

3. **Athlete** ____   c. Nameless

4. **Biology** ____   d. Love of knowledge

5. **Astronomy** ____   e. Competitor for a prize

78

Answer key on page 233.

Greek Crisscross

Can you fit all ten of the following Greek gods into the puzzle below, without any clues?

**Aphrodite • Apollo • Ares • Artemis • Athena
Demeter • Hera • Hermes • Poseidon • Zeus**

Answer key on page 233.

Code Breaker

Use these letters from the Greek alphabet to discover how Annie describes those around her.

α=a δ=d ε=e ι=i κ=k μ=m

ν=n π=p ρ=r σ=s τ=t υ=y

Jack is _____.
σ μ α ρ τ

Pegasus is _____.
π ρ ε τ τ υ

Morgan is _____.
κ ι ν δ

80

Answer key on page 233.

Tonight on the *Titanic*

Maze

Help the passengers find their way to the deck of the *Titanic*.

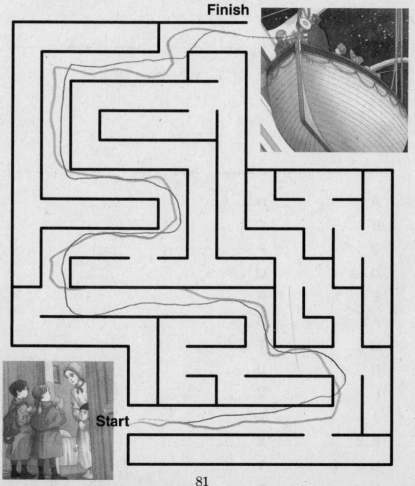

Finish

Start

Answer key on page 234.

Code Breaker

Morse code is an international form of communication that was used when the *Titanic* was launched. Using the alphabet key below, see if you can decipher the following message to the captain of the *Titanic*.

‾‾ ⋅‾ ‾ ‾⋅‾⋅ ⋅⋅⋅⋅ ‾‾‾ ⋅⋅‾ ‾

W A T C H O U T

⋅⋅‾⋅ ‾‾‾ ⋅‾⋅

F O R

⋅⋅ ‾⋅‾⋅ ⋅ ‾⋅⋅⋅ ⋅ ⋅‾⋅ ‾‾⋅ ⋅⋅⋅

I C E B E R G S.

A ._		**N** _.
B _...		**O** _ _ _
C _._.		**P** ._ _.
D _..		**Q** _ _._
E .		**R** ._.
F .._.		**S** ...
G _ _.		**T** _
H		**U** .._
I ..		**V** ..._
J ._ _ _		**W** ._ _
K _._		**X** _.._
L ._..		**Y** _._ _
M _ _		**Z** _ _..

Answer key on page 234.

Connect-the-Dots

Start at 1, and connect the dots to see who joins Jack and Annie on their adventure in *Tonight on the* Titanic.

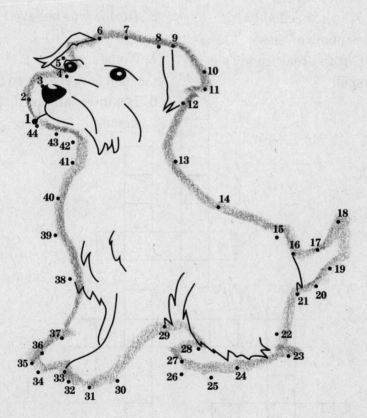

Answer key on page 234.

Crossword Puzzle

Use the clues for Across and Down to fill in the puzzle spaces.

ACROSS

3. The nearest ship turned off this
5. *Titanic* needed twice as many of these
7. Gift to break Teddy's spell

DOWN

1. Boy whom Jack and Annie save
2. *Titanic* was believed to be this
4. Women and children were saved _____
6. The international distress signal

Answer key on page 234.

Compass Game

Rewrite history! The captain of the *Titanic* needs your help to complete his directions for navigating through the ice field. Using the map and compass, fill in the missing information to guide the ship to safety.

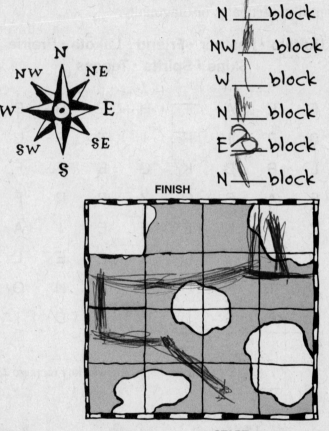

N ___ block

NW ___ block

W ___ block

N ___ block

E ___ block

N ___ block

FINISH

START

Answer key on page 234.

Buffalo Before Breakfast

Word Search

Find and circle the words below. Words can go horizontally, vertically, or diagonally.

**Buffalo · Feather · Friend · Lakota · Prairie
Skins · Spirits · Tepees**

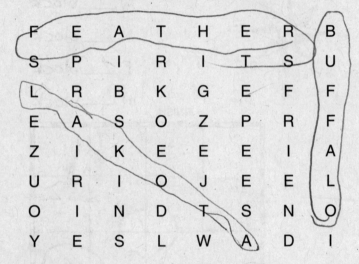

```
F  E  A  T  H  E  R  R  B
S  P  I  R  I  T  S  S  U
L  R  B  K  G  E  F  F  F
E  A  S  O  Z  P  R  R  F
Z  I  K  E  E  E  I  A
U  R  I  O  J  E  E  L
O  I  N  D  T  S  N  O
Y  E  S  L  W  A  D  I
```

Answer key on page 234.

Illustrate It!

Jack and Annie are amazed to learn that tepees were made of buffalo skins and that the Lakota honored the buffalo for giving them food, shelter, and clothing. Draw and decorate a Lakota tepee with designs of your own.

Lakota Name

Jack and Annie meet a Lakota boy named Black Hawk and receive their Lakota names based on their actions. Annie is Buffalo Girl, and Jack is Rides-Like-Wind. What would your Lakota name be? Write it on the line below and decorate the page.

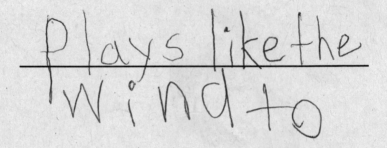

Plays like the Wind to

Waste Not, Want Not

The Lakota people used every part of a buffalo's body so that nothing was wasted. Help Jack and Annie match each material on the left with the object that the Lakota people would make with it.

1. **Muscle** —— a. Tools

2. **Skin** —— b. Sleds

3. **Bones** —— c. Food

4. **Horns** —— d. Ropes

5. **Hair** —— e. Cups

6. **Ribs** —— f. Tepee

Answer key on page 234.

Triangle Mystery

Color in each three-sided shape to reveal the true name for buffalo.

Answer key on page 235.

Tigers at Twilight

Vanity-Plate Puzzler

License plates have combinations of eight or fewer numbers and letters to keep track of who owns which car. On long car rides, you'll sometimes spot funny license plates with messages on them. These license plates are called vanity plates because people use them to tell others about themselves. See if you can figure out who the vanity plates below would belong to.

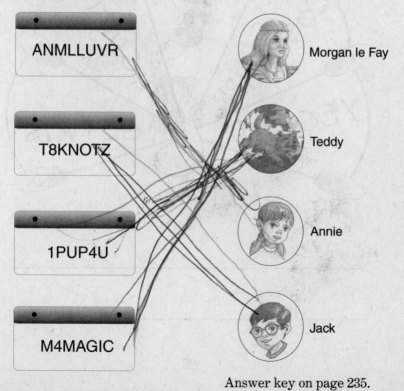

ANMLLUVR

T8KNOTZ

1PUP4U

M4MAGIC

Morgan le Fay

Teddy

Annie

Jack

Answer key on page 235.

Peacock Puzzle

Jack and Annie see lots of animals in the jungle when they get their gift from a forest far away. This peacock has a message for them—each feather is a word, but the letters are scrambled! See if you can figure out the message, and write it on the line below.

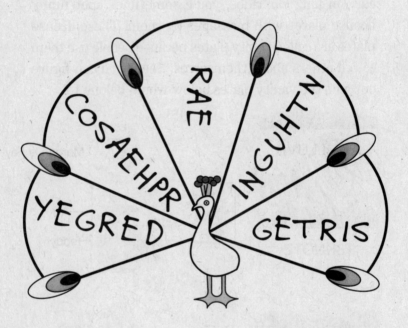

_____

_____.

Answer key on page 235.

Crossword Puzzle

Use the clues for Across and Down to fill in the puzzle spaces.

ACROSS

3. Word that means "having a long tail"
4. Tigers sharpen these on tree trunks
5. Pythons are not this

DOWN

1. A faraway place where Jack and Annie find a gift
2. Jack thinks rhinos need these
3. The hermit's gift

Answer key on page 235.

Python Puzzle

Jack and Annie learn that pythons aren't poisonous snakes, but they squeeze their prey to death and swallow it whole! Start at this python's head and cross out any letters in the word "monkey" to complete the joke below.

What did the python say to Jack?

I have a C̶R̶u̶s̶h̶ _____ on you!

Answer key on page 235.

Listen!

The hermit tells Jack and Annie that he has listened to nature for so long, the sounds have become "one great voice of the forest." Close your eyes and listen to the world around you. Then open your eyes and write down the first four things you hear where you are right now.

1. Air cindisaner

2. Dada and cece

3. Mom Macking Moring Brektest

4. _____

Dingoes at Dinnertime

Habitat Match

Jack and Annie see so many different things on their travels, they sometimes have trouble remembering where they saw what! See if you can remember where Jack and Annie saw the following by matching each with its proper habitat. You can use each habitat more than once.

America   India   Australia

1. bison _____

2. kookaburras _____

3. peacocks _____

4. ponies _____

5. kangaroos _____

6. koalas _____

7. tigers _____

8. emus _____

9. rhinoceroses _____

10. pythons _____

Answer key on page 235.

Matching

In Australia, Jack and Annie learn that the kookaburra makes a strange sound that reminds people of a braying donkey. Circle the two kookaburra birds that are exactly the same.

Answer key on page 236.

Dreamtime Magic

The Rainbow Serpent sends rain to Jack and Annie because they touch the handprints that the Aborigines have painted on the magic snake. Trace your handprint below and decorate it to make it magical like the Aboriginal handprints.

Gum Tree Tangle

Koalas rarely drink water. They get moisture from the leaves they eat. Which one of these three koalas makes it to the gum tree? The first

Answer key on page 236.

Break the Spell!

Jack and Annie have finally collected all four gifts to break Teddy's spell. Help Morgan match each gift to its part of the rhyme by drawing the gifts in the boxes.

A gift from a ship lost at sea.

A gift from the prairie blue.

A gift from a forest far away.

A gift from a kangaroo.

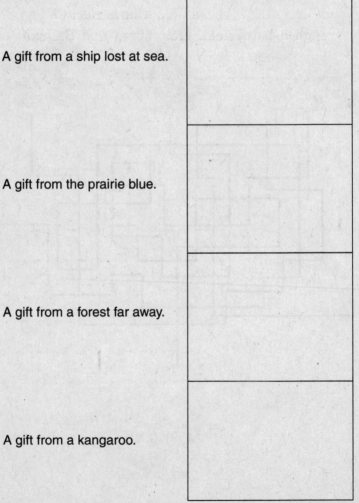

Answer key on page 236.

Civil War on Sunday

Maze

Jack and Annie must help Clara Barton travel through a battlefield! Help them find the safest route back to the field hospital.

Finish

Start

Answer key on page 236.

Musical Notes

Drummer boys were very important in the Civil War. As Jack and Annie learned, their drumbeats communicated with soldiers on smoky battlefields. Find the hidden message in the musical notes below! A vertical line means a space between words.

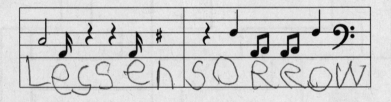

Confederate Crisscross

Eleven states fought for the Confederacy in the Civil War. See if you can figure out all eleven by looking at the map and fitting their names into the grid below.

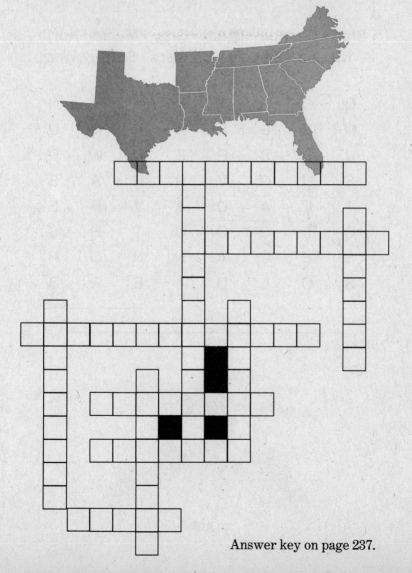

Answer key on page 237.

Word Search

Find and circle the words below. Words can go horizontally, vertically, or diagonally. The letters you don't circle will spell out a hidden message!

Blue · Cannon · Drum · Gray · Music · North
Nurses · Slavery · Soldiers · South · War

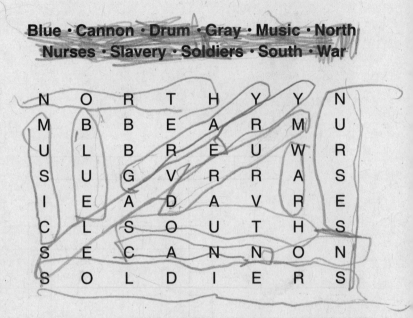

```
N  O  R  T  H  Y  Y  N
M  B  B  E  A  R  M  U
U  L  B  R  E  U  W  R
S  U  G  V  R  R  A  S
I  E  A  D  A  V  R  E
C  L  S  O  U  T  H  S
S  E  C  A  N  N  O  N
S  O  L  D  I  E  R  S
```

_____.

Answer key on page 237.

Family Tree

When they visit a Civil War battlefield, Jack and Annie meet their great-great-great-grandfather. He is a brave kid, just like them!

Fill out the family tree below. With help from an adult in your family, write one adjective to describe each of your grandparents and parents. Then write any of those adjectives that describe you, too. Do you take after your relatives?

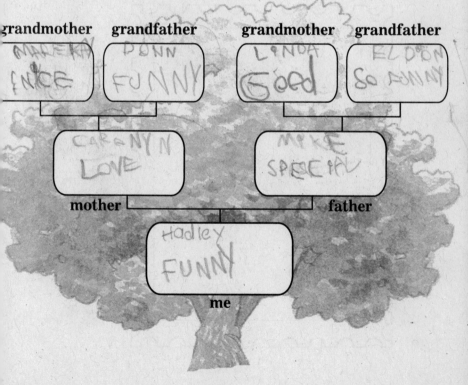

grandmother   grandfather   grandmother   grandfather

MALEKA — NICE

DONN — FUNNY

LINDA — Good

ELDON — So FUNNY

CAROLYN — LOVE

MIKE — SPECIAL

mother   father

Hadley — FUNNY

me

Revolutionary War on Wednesday

Illustrate It!

The Stamp Act made the colonists very angry. Design a stamp showing an event of the Revolutionary War.

Fill in the Blanks

In *Revolutionary War on Wednesday*, George Washington thanks Jack and Annie for their help. Fill in the blanks to draft a thank-you note that Washington may have written to thank a soldier for his war efforts.

Dear _____Denny_____,

Thank you for your service during the Revolutionary War.

I especially want to thank you for _____your_____ _____anger and_____ and your willingness to _____secused_____ _____and think that r will win_____.

I know that the other soldiers appreciate your _____conoge_____ and bravery, too.

Best wishes upon your return to _____saftty home_____.

Sincerely and with thanks,
George Washington

Code Breaker

In one of the most famous events of the Revolutionary War, a light was set in a lighthouse. It was a simple code: one light if the British came by land, two lights if they came by sea. Imagine that the patriots needed to send a more complicated message using flashing lights to communicate in Morse code. Use the key below to decipher the important message!

Morse Code Alphabet Key

A	. _	N	_ .
B	_ . . .	O	_ _ _
C	_ . _ .	P	. _ _ .
D	_ . .	Q	_ _ . _
E	.	R	. _ .
F	. . _ .	S	. . .
G	_ _ .	T	_
H	. . . .	U	. . _
I	. .	V	. . . _
J	. _ _ _	W	. _ _
K	_ . _	X	_ . . _
L	. _ . .	Y	_ . _ _
M	_ _	Z	_ _ . .

_ .... .   _... .-. .. _ ... .
T h   e   B   R   I T S   H

.- .-. .   -.-. --- -- .. -. --.
A R E   C   O   M I N G

The BRITISH ARE COMING!

Answer key on page 237.

Compass Game

Imagine that you are in charge of navigating one of George Washington's boats across the Delaware River. You have a map. There are three possible places to dock on the opposite bank, but only one of them will help you surprise the enemy. Use your compass to complete your mission safely.

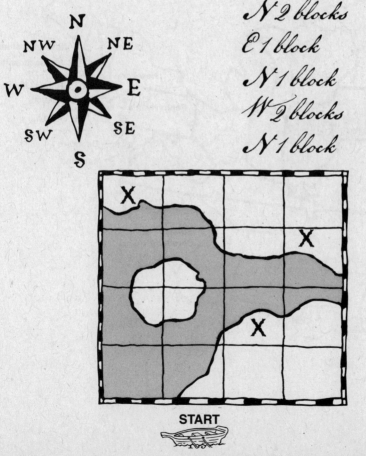

N 2 blocks
E 1 block
N 1 block
W 2 blocks
N 1 block

START

Answer key on page 237.

Matching

The Thirteen Colonies are now all states. Can you match each state to its nickname?

New Hampshire

Massachusetts

New York

Rhode Island

Connecticut

Pennsylvania

New Jersey

Delaware

Maryland

Virginia

North Carolina

South Carolina

Georgia

1. **Connecticut** _____ a. Bay State

2. **Delaware** _____ b. Constitution State

3. **Georgia** _____ c. Empire State

4. **Maryland** _____ d. First State

5. **Massachusetts** _____ e. Free State

6. **New Hampshire** _____ f. Garden State

7. **New Jersey** _____ g. Granite State

8. **New York** _____ h. Keystone State

9. **North Carolina** _____ i. Ocean State

10. **Pennsylvania** _____ j. Old Dominion State

11. **Rhode Island** _____ k. Palmetto State

12. **South Carolina** _____ l. Peach State

13. **Virginia** _____ m. Tar Heel State

111

Answer key on page 237.

Twister on Tuesday

Railroad Crossing

All aboard for a trip to California! But which one of these three trains will take you coast to coast?

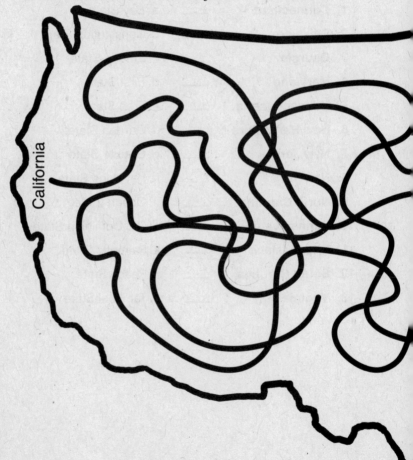

California

Answer key on page 238.

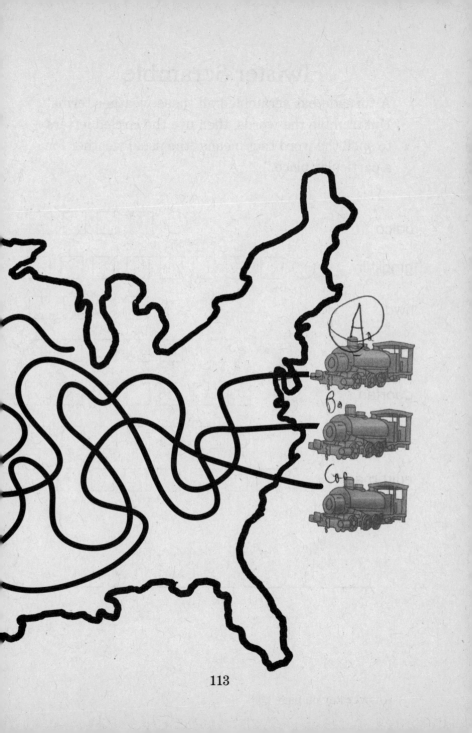

Twister Scramble

A tornado has scrambled all these weather terms! Unscramble the words, then use the circled letters to spell the word that means "the usual weather for a particular place."

udlco   ⬡ ▢ ▢ ▢ ▢

gtngiihln   ⬡ ▢ ▢ ▢ ▢ ▢ ▢ ▢ ▢

nwdi   ▢ ⬡ ▢ ▢

morts   ▢ ▢ ▢ ▢ ⬡

doortan   ▢ ▢ ▢ ▢ ⬡ ▢ ▢

ntrehud   ⬡ ▢ ▢ ▢ ▢ ▢ ▢

cuirhrnae   ▢ ▢ ▢ ▢ ▢ ▢ ▢ ▢ ⬡

___ ___ ___ ___ ___ ___ ___

Answer key on page 238.

Time and Time Again

Jack and Annie have made two separate journeys to the prairie. Draw a line to match the following objects to the appropriate time period.

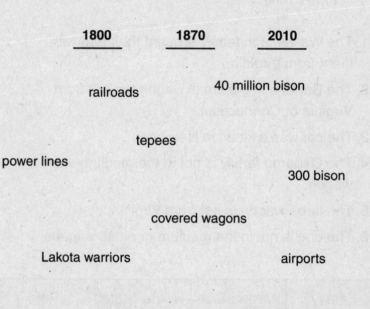

1800	1870	2010

railroads

40 million bison

tepees

power lines

300 bison

covered wagons

Lakota warriors

airports

dugouts

hospitals

Answer key on page 238.

Logic Puzzle

Three covered wagons are traveling across the prairie. Read the clues below to figure out the size of each family's wagon, the pet they have with them, and what state they are from. Use the grid to help you figure it out!

1. The Washington family brought their bird with them from Virginia.
2. The Bartons in the small wagon are not from Virginia or Connecticut.
3. The cat was a kitten in New York.
4. The Osborne family is not in the medium-sized wagon.
5. The large wagon is not from Virginia.
6. The dog is not in the medium or small wagons.

Family	Wagon Size	Home State	Pet
Osbornes			
Washingtons			
Bartons			

Answer key on page 238.

Vortex Riddle

You're staring into the vortex of a terrifying twister! The twister has sucked up the answer to a riddle. Start on the outside and work to the center of the vortex. Write down only every other letter. When you get to the center, go back in the other direction and write down the letters you didn't get the first time.

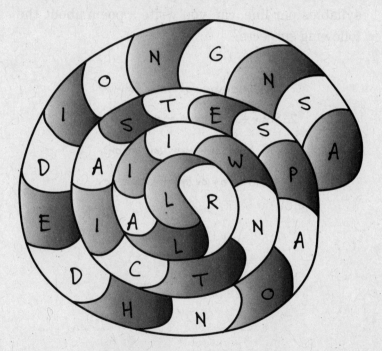

Why does Annie carry a leash with her umbrella?

_____.

Answer key on page 238.

Earthquake in the Early Morning
Words of Wisdom

Jack and Annie recover a poem from the Great Earthquake of 1906. Using the same number of syllables per line, can you write a poem about the following subjects?

1. A member of your family

2. Your favorite subject in school

3. Your summer vacation

4. A hobby or sport you enjoy

THERE IS NO WATER
AND STILL LESS SOAP,
WE HAVE NO CITY,
BUT LOTS OF HOPE.

Dynamite Duel

Find a friend, sibling, or parent and challenge him or her to a battle for the city. One of you is a raging fire, spreading from building to building. The other player is a firefighter, saving buildings. Take turns drawing lines connecting the buildings, one line at a time, to make a square. Lines can go horizontally or vertically, but not diagonally. The player who completes a square wins that city block and gets to put his or her initial inside it and take another turn. The player with more city blocks wins. Jack has made the first move here.

Journalism Challenge

Jack and Annie talk to a reporter after they experience the Great Earthquake. If you could be a journalist at any time in history, what period would you choose? What person from that period would you want to interview? Ask a friend or family member to pose as that person. Then conduct an interview and write down the best answers.

Split Compounds

A tremendous earthquake has split these words in two! Can you put them back together? Hint: All the answers are compound words that appear in *Earthquake in the Early Morning.*

1. some	——	a.	quake
2. school	——	b.	stone
3. back	——	c.	foot
4. news	——	d.	paper
5. arm	——	e.	load
6. cobble	——	f.	thing
7. gas	——	g.	light
8. bare	——	h.	house
9. earth	——	i.	pack

Answer key on page 238.

City Crisscross

San Francisco is a large city with many neighbor-hoods. Can you fit all ten of these neighborhoods into the puzzle below without any clues? Ignore spaces and punctuation when filling in the puzzle.

Chinatown • Fisherman's Wharf • Haight • Marina Mission • Nob Hill • Noe Valley • North Beach SoMa • Union Square

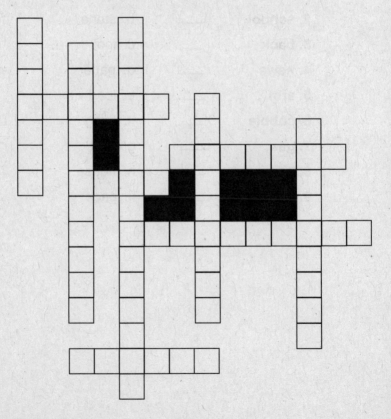

Answer key on page 238.

Stage Fright on a Summer Night

Word Search

Find and circle the words below. Words can go horizontally, vertically, or diagonally.

**Bear · Bow · Costume · London
Onstage · Queen · Theater · Will**

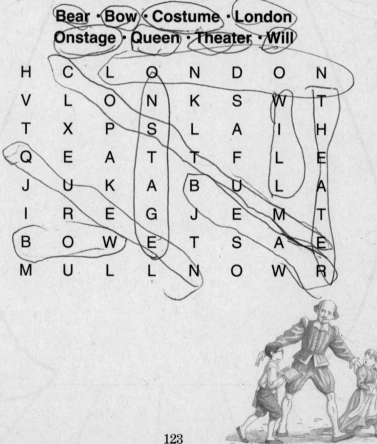

```
H  C  L  O  N  D  O  N     N
V  L  O  N  K  S  W     T
T  X  P  S  L  A  I     H
Q  E  A  T  T  F  L     E
J  U  K  A  B  U  L     A
I  R  E  G  J  E  M     T
B  O  W  E  T  S  A  E
M  U  L  L  N  O  W  R
```

Answer key on page 239.

Illustrate It!

Jack and Annie perform in William Shakespeare's play *A Midsummer Night's Dream.* Draw yourself on the stage below.

Read the Part

Jack is nervous about reading onstage, but Will Shakespeare tells him that if he believes he is in the forest on a summer night, the audience will believe it, too. See if you can read the part clearly and with feeling.

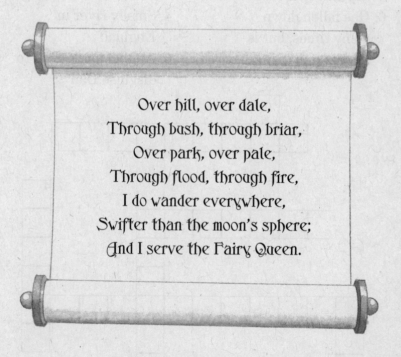

Over hill, over dale,
Through bush, through briar,
Over park, over pale,
Through flood, through fire,
I do wander everywhere,
Swifter than the moon's sphere;
And I serve the Fairy Queen.

Crossword Puzzle

Use the clues for Across and Down to fill in the puzzle spaces.

ACROSS

2. Queen of England in 1600
5. Magic that turns daytime into night
6. Has fallen down many times, but is always built again

DOWN

1. William Shakespeare's theater
3. Place people watched bears fight with dogs
4. Smelly river in England
6. Animal mask used to disguise Dan

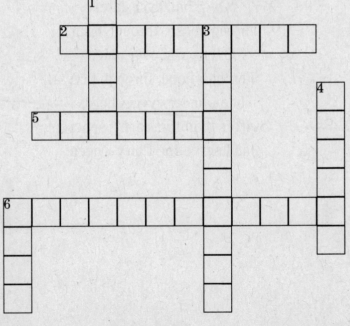

Answer key on page 239.

Costume Fun

Jack and "Andy" have been asked to be in another play by William Shakespeare. Design the costumes they should wear.

Good Morning, Gorillas

Maze

Help Jack find Annie when they get separated in the misty rain forest in the mountains of central Africa.

Finish

Start

128

Answer key on page 239.

Connect-the-Dots

Start at 1, and connect the dots to see whom Jack learns from in *Good Morning, Gorillas*.

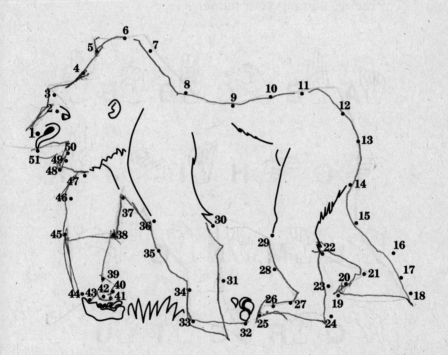

Answer key on page 239.

A Special Language

Jack and Annie learn that gorillas are very intelligent and can understand sign language. American Sign Language is a special language using hand gestures. It is used by people who are unable to hear. Below is the American Sign Language alphabet. Practice signing your name.

Sign Language Code

Use the sign language alphabet on the previous page to decode the message below.

Answer key on page 239.

Gorilla Diet Scramble

A silverback gorilla can eat up to fifty pounds of forest vegetation in one day. Unscramble the words to learn what gorillas usually eat. Then unscramble the letters in the circles to find out what gorillas do *not* usually eat.

sevale ☐ ☐ ◯ ☐ ☐ ☐

gsitw ◯ ☐ ☐ ☐ ☐

sfwlore ☐ ☐ ☐ ☐ ◯ ☐ ☐

bmoboa ☐ ☐ ◯ ☐ ☐ ☐

◯ ◯ ◯ ◯

Answer key on page 240.

Thanksgiving on Thursday

Your Thanksgiving

In 1863, President Lincoln made Thanksgiving a national holiday. Since then, families and friends celebrate Thanksgiving each year. What does your family do on Thanksgiving? Do you have any special traditions? What do you give thanks for?

_____

_____

_____

_____

Which Magic Tree House Character Are You?

Answer the questions below to discover which Magic Tree House character you would be!

1. What instrument would you like to play?
   - a. Violin
   - b. Trumpet
   - c. No instrument, I would be the conductor.

2. What would you like to be when you grow up?
   - a. Actor
   - b. Newspaper reporter
   - c. Teacher

3. Which saying do you agree with the most?
   - a. Many hands make light work.
   - b. Nothing ventured, nothing gained.
   - c. Look before you leap.

4. Which animal would you like to be?
   - a. Penguin
   - b. Stag
   - c. Dolphin

Answer key on page 240.

Crossword Puzzle

Use the clues for Across and Down to fill in the puzzle spaces.

ACROSS

3. Federation of Native American tribes that made peace with the Pilgrims
5. Clam that lives sixty years or more
6. Jack burns this bird

DOWN

1. Carried the Pilgrims from England to America in 1620
2. Important plant to the Pilgrims
4. Native American who helped the Pilgrims survive

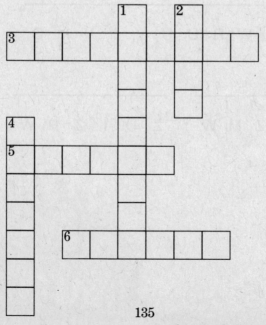

Answer key on page 240.

Code Breaker

Use the reverse alphabet code (A = Z, B = Y, C = X, and so on) to help Jack and Annie discover Squanto's message.

_____   _____   _____
Y V   P R M W   G L

_____   _____   _____
G S L H V   D S L   U V V O

_____
W R U U V I V M G

_____   _____ .
Z M W   Z U I Z R W

Answer key on page 240.

Say Again?

Jack and Annie learn that the Pilgrims caught eels by pushing them out of the sand with their bare feet and then catching them with their hands. Draw speech bubbles or thought bubbles and write in what Jack and Annie are saying or thinking at this point in the story.

High Tide in Hawaii

Illustrate It!

Kama and Boka teach Jack and Annie how to surf.
Draw yourself learning to surf below.

Maze

Jack and Annie learn that tsunamis are created when earthquakes or volcanoes push a huge amount of seawater up from the ocean floor. The water rises higher and higher until it hits the shore in a gigantic wave that washes everything away. Help Jack, Annie, Kama, and Boka escape the tsunami.

Finish

Start

Answer key on page 240.

Word Search

Find and circle the words below. Words can go horizontally, vertically, or diagonally.

**Hula · Island · Paradise · Poi
Surf · Taro · Tsunamis · Volcano**

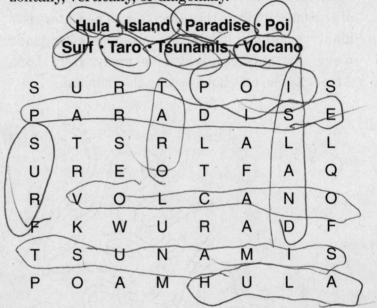

```
S  U  R  T  P  O  I  S
P  A  R  A  D  I  S  E
S  T  S  R  L  A  L  L
U  R  E  O  T  F  A  Q
R  V  O  L  C  A  N  O
F  K  W  U  R  A  D  F
T  S  U  N  A  M  I  S
P  O  A  M  H  U  L  A
```

Answer key on page 240.

Hula Dance

Jack and Annie learn that early Hawaiians had no written language. They told stories with hula dancing. See if you can create a hula dance about Hawaii. Make sure you include these facts in your story, and don't forget to make your hips sway!

- The Hawaiian islands were formed millions of years ago by volcanoes.

- The volcanoes erupted under the ocean. Over time, their craters rose above the water.

- Wind and birds dropped seeds on the islands. These became plants.

- About two thousand years ago, people came to Hawaii in canoes from other Pacific islands.

- They paddled for thousands of miles across the ocean, guided only by the wind and stars.

Matching

In Hawaii, Jack and Annie use simple wooden surfboards. Today, people usually ride decorated boards made of resin and fiberglass. Circle the two surfboards that are exactly the same.

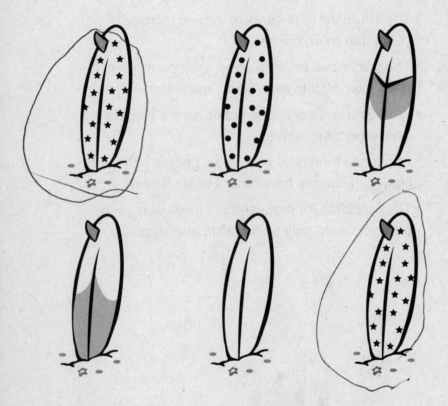

Answer key on page 240.

Christmas in Camelot

Knight Crisscross

Can you fit these Knights of the Round Table into the puzzle below? All the letters in the word "knight" have been provided for you.

**Bedivere • Bors • Galahad • Gawain
Kay • Lancelot • Percival • Tristram**

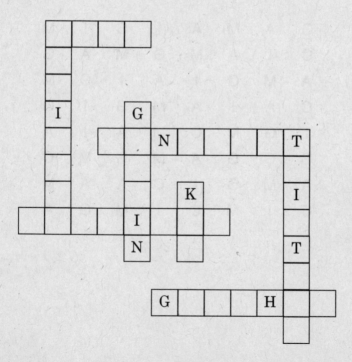

Answer key on page 241.

Hidden Magic

Even when King Arthur bans all magic in Camelot, a little bit of magic remains—thanks to Merlin the Magician. Can you find the word "magic" in the grid below? It might appear going up or down, backward or forward, or even diagonally. But it only appears once!

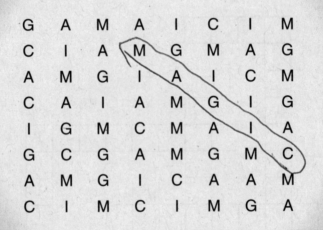

```
G  A  M  A  A  I  C  I  M
C  I  A  M  G  M  A  G
A  M  G  I  A  I  C  M
C  A  I  A  M  G  I  G
I  G  M  C  M  A  I  A
G  C  G  A  M  G  M  C
A  M  G  I  C  A  A  M
C  I  M  C  I  M  G  A
```

Answer key on page 241.

What If?

Memory and imagination are two key ingredients for good stories. Try writing one yourself! Remember something that has happened in your life. Start writing the true story. But imagine that something went differently. What might have happened then? Write out one possibility, and you've written a story!

Word Search

Jack and Annie have encountered some fantastic people and creatures in their travels. Find and circle the examples below. Words can go horizontally, vertically, or diagonally. And the tricky "elf" appears twice! The letters you don't circle will tell you where all of these people and creatures come from.

**Dragon · Elf · Fairy · Ghost
Magician · Monster · Selkie · Unicorn**

M	A	G	I	C	I	A	N
M	F	T	H	F	E	E	U
O	A	I	L	M	I	N	N
N	I	E	A	K	O	G	I
S	R	I	L	G	N	F	C
T	Y	E	A	A	L	T	O
E	S	R	I	E	O	N	R
R	D	G	H	O	S	T	N

They come from _____ _____.

Answer key on page 241.

Rhyme Time

Below are the words to a song that Jack and Annie sing to each other. Use your knowledge of rhyming to guess what the missing words might be.

You're the cornflakes
I'm the milk
You're the silkworm
I'm the _____
You're the saddle
I'm the stirrup
You're the pancakes
I'm the _____
I'm the peaches
You're the cream
What would I do without you?
We're a _____!

Answer key on page 241.

Haunted Castle on Hallows Eve

Illustrate It!

The Raven King has the body of a man and the head of a bird. He gives Jack and Annie a scare! Turn the tables by creating something that could scare the Raven King. What do you think he would be afraid of?

Logic Puzzle

Jack, Annie, and Teddy are all going trick-or-treating. Their costumes are so good that it's hard to tell who's who! Read the clues below to figure out each kid's costume, what color the costume is, and what each kid is using to carry candy. Use the grid to help you figure it out!

1. Annie is too afraid of spiders to dress like one.
2. Jack's costume is purple.
3. Teddy is not carrying his candy in a pumpkin or a pillowcase.
4. The kid dressed like a dog is carrying a basket.
5. The kid carrying a pillowcase is wearing a black costume.
6. The bird costume is not brown.

Kid	Costume	Carrying	Color
Jack			
Annie			
Teddy			

149

Answer key on page 241.

Code Breaker

Use the reverse alphabet code (A = Z, B = Y, C = X, and so on) to help Jack and Annie figure out what to do when they are accidentally transformed into birds.

_____   _____

G S V B   H S L F O W

_____   _____   _____.

Q F H G   D R M T   R G

Answer key on page 241.

Optical Illusion

Merlin is up to his old tricks. He's hidden a message in the image below. Hold this page at eye level and tilt it back slowly until you can read what he has written. (Hint: The letters are in black.) Can you make a message of your own using the same trick?

Answer key on page 241.

Math Puzzle

Jack and Annie have left a bag of candy for their friends in Camelot. Follow the clues to discover how many pieces of candy each person gets.

1. There are 20 pieces of candy in all.

2. Morgan le Fay has known Jack and Annie the longest, so she gets half the candy.

3. Teddy and Kathleen get the same amount of candy.

4. Kathleen has 2 more pieces of candy than Merlin does.

5. Teddy has twice as much candy as Merlin.

Morgan gets ___ pieces.

Merlin gets ___ pieces.

Teddy gets ___ pieces.

Kathleen gets ___ pieces.

Answer key on page 241.

MAGIC TREE HOUSE® #31

Summer of the
Sea Serpent

Maze

Help Jack and Annie climb the web of the Spider
Queen—without getting stuck!

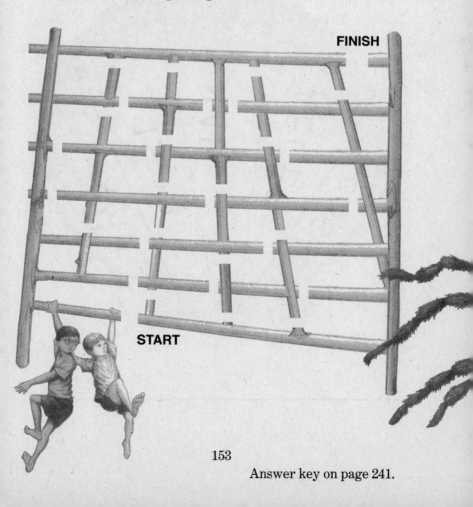

153

Answer key on page 241.

Shell Scramble

Merlin has left a message for Jack and Annie on the seashell below, but the Ice Wizard has scrambled every word of it. Help Jack and Annie figure out what the message is supposed to say.

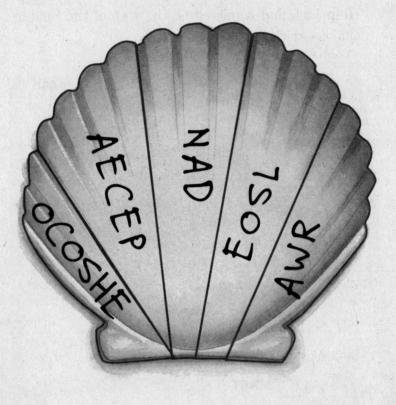

_____.

Rhyme Time

Teddy is a sorcerer in training, but he sometimes has trouble making his spells rhyme. Can you help him out with the following spells?

Over the sea,
Through the air,
Help me travel

_____!

On cloudy day
Or blackest night,
Candles, shine true

_____!

When I am trapped,
I must be free.
Change now into

_____!

Answer key on page 242.

Matching

Jack and Annie are looking for the mythical sword Excalibur. But there are fake copies right next to the real thing! Circle the real sword, which is not like any of the others below.

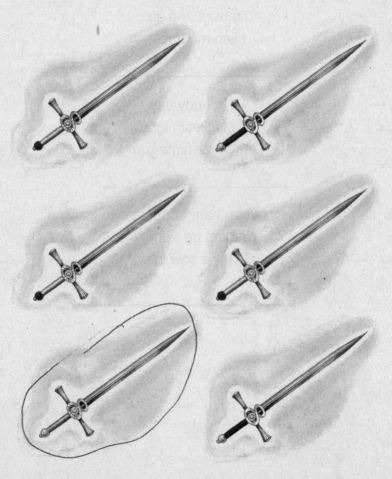

Answer key on page 242.

Illustrate It!

In *Summer of the Sea Serpent,* Jack and Annie encounter a creature that is half horse and half fish. Make your own animal mix-ups with a friend or family member! Follow the steps below.

1. Fold a piece of paper in half.
2. Draw the top half of any animal's body on one side of the folded paper. You should draw the head down to the stomach area, and the stomach area should end along the folded edge of the paper.
3. Turn the paper over. Make little marks where your drawing ends, so that the two half-drawings will combine to make a single creature.
4. Have your partner draw the bottom half of any animal. Don't tell your partner what animal you chose for the top half!
5. When your partner has finished, unfold the paper to see what crazy combination you have created.
6. Give your creation a name!

Winter of the Ice Wizard

Scrambled Speech

The letters below are scrambled, but they are in the correct columns. Figure out where to place each letter to write out words of wisdom from Merlin to Jack and Annie.

W	H	E	N	F	T	O	S	A	G	A	B	S	H
I	I	N	T	O	R		I	E	H	I	A	U	T
T	S	N		E	R		R	T	L	R	R	N	T

Answer key on page 242.

Snowflake Similarities

No two snowflakes are supposed to look exactly alike. But when you're in a land of myth and magic, science doesn't always apply! Look at the snowflakes below. Circle the two that are the same.

Answer key on page 242.

Winter Scramble

A snowstorm has scrambled all these wintry terms!
Unscramble the words, then use the circled letters
to answer the question: Why did the Ice Wizard's
sister stop talking to him?

wnos   Ⓢ ⃞n ⃞o ⃞w

ihla   Ⓗⓐ ⃞i ⃞l

docl   ⃞c Ⓞ ⃞l ⃞d

doudl   ⃞c ⃞l Ⓞ Ⓤ ⃞d

tesel   Ⓢ ⃞l ⓔ ⓔ ⃞t

xdnrplak   ⃞b ⃞l ⃞i ⃞z ⃞z ⃞a ⃞r Ⓓ

ecl   Ⓘ ⃞c ⓔ

stolf   ⃞f ⃞r ⃞o Ⓢ ⃞t

S h c a l d e r

Answer: She wanted to give him the cold shcalder !

160

Answer key on page 242.

Tangled Weaving

The three Fates are weaving a story about Jack and Annie, but their threads are getting all tangled up! Follow the thread that leads to a happy ending at the magic tree house.

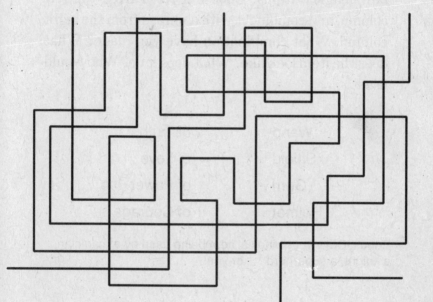

Answer key on page 243.

Magical Mix-up

Jack and Annie collected four magical items for Merlin: the Water of Memory and Imagination, the Diamond of Destiny, the Sword of Light, and the Staff of Strength. Now it's time to make entirely new magical items. Choose a word from the left column, and combine it with a phrase from the right column. What combination have you made? What does the item look like? What does it do? Who would use it?

Wand	of Truth
Shield	of Love
Gem	of Power
Helmet	of Courage

Bonus: Draw your magical item being used by a magician, a knight, a superhero . . . or you!

Carnival at Candlelight

Illustrate It!

For the yearly festival of Carnival in Venice, people disguise themselves as anything they want to be. Draw yourself into this Carnival scene as anything *you* want to be.

Spot the Differences

Look at the picture on top. Then look at the picture on the bottom and circle the five differences.

Answer key on page 243.

Maze

The prison cells at ground level in the palace were called *pozzi,* meaning "wells" or "pits." Help Jack and Annie escape the *pozzi.*

Finish

Start

Answer key on page 243.

Clock Puzzle

Venice has been called a timeless city. These clocks have letters instead of numbers. Draw in the hands to indicate the times written beneath each clock. The hands point to the letters you need to write Merlin's message below.

6:45

12:15

3:30

9:00

6:15

12:00

Answer key on page 243.

Triangle Mystery

Color in each three-sided shape to reveal the symbol of Neptune.

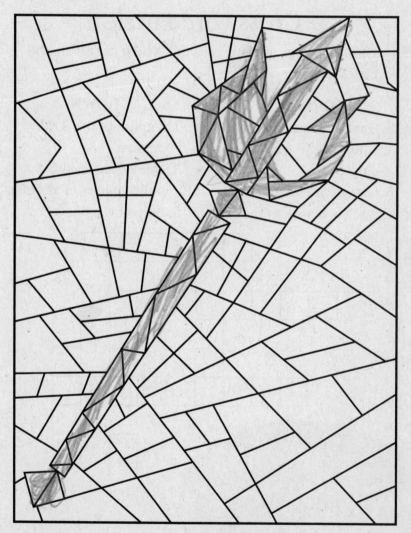

Answer key on page 244.

Season of the Sandstorms

Crossword Puzzle

Use the clues for Across and Down to fill in the puzzle spaces.

ACROSS

2. Open-air market
4. Ruler of the Arab empire
6. Causes travelers to lose their way in the desert

DOWN

1. Capital of the Arab empire
3. One of the greatest philosophers of all time
5. Ship of the desert

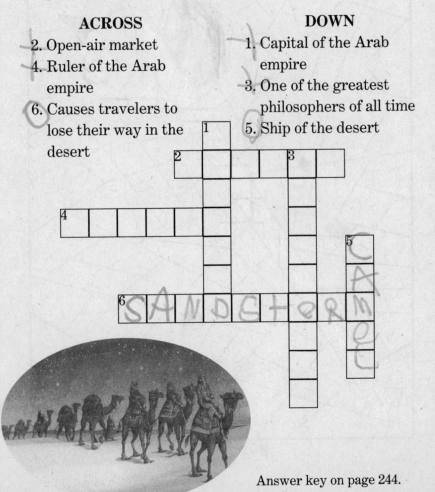

Answer key on page 244.

Camel Confusion

Camels can travel one hundred miles in a single day. Which of these camels will find its way to Jack after the sandstorm?

Answer key on page 244.

Mystic Math

Jack and Annie get to see al-Khwarizmi, the man who perfected Arabic numerals. Use the Arabic numerals below to solve math problems. Each problem gives a number. Each number equals a letter in the alphabet (A = 1, B = 2, C = 3, and so on). Unscramble the answers to find out how the world grows wise.

$$12 - 4 =$$
$$2 + 3 =$$
$$15 - 11 =$$

$$9 + 9 =$$
$$7 - 6 =$$
$$5 + 14 =$$

When wisdom is _____.

Answer key on page 244.

Book Battle

Find a friend, sibling, or parent and challenge him or her to a battle to study more books. Take turns drawing lines connecting the books, one line at a time, to make a square. Lines can go horizontally or vertically, but not diagonally. The player who completes a square gets to put his or her initial inside it and take another turn. The player with more squares wins. Jack has made the first move here.

Illustrate It!

The book of Aristotle's writings was a treasure. Inside the treasure chest, draw a picture of your favorite character from your favorite book.

Night of the New Magicians

Word Search

Find and circle the words below. Words can go horizontally, vertically, or diagonally.

Bulb · Eiffel · Genius · Invent
Phone · Study · Vaccine · Work

W	E	I	F	F	E	L	R
P	V	I	N	V	E	N	T
H	S	A	C	X	G	E	N
O	T	M	C	T	E	P	W
N	U	I	E	C	N	I	O
E	D	P	H	U	I	S	R
M	Y	F	O	Y	U	N	K
B	U	L	B	J	S	C	E

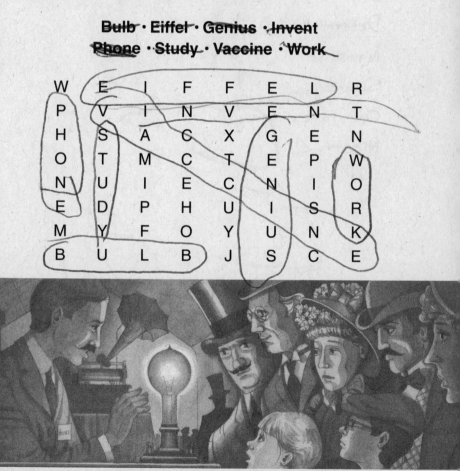

Answer key on page 244.

More Than a Name

Jack and Annie have created an acrostic poem out of Edison's name. Use the space provided to write your name vertically. Then write words that describe you that begin with the letters of your name.

Engineer

Determined

Inquisitive

Smart

Open to new ideas

Nice

Scrambled Scientists

Jack and Annie learned many new things on their adventure at the 1889 World's Fair. Write in the answers in the spaces provided. Then unscramble the letters in the circles to spell the kind of magic the new magicians practiced.

1. The inventor of the lightbulb.

   ☐ ☐ ◯ ☐ ◯

2. The inventor of the telephone.

   ☐ ◯ ☐ ☐

3. Another word for the tiny particles we call germs.

   ☐ ☐ ◯ ☐ ☐ ☐ ◯ ☐

4. A doctor whose research led to many medicines and vaccines.

   ☐ ☐ ◯ ☐ ☐ ☐ ☐

5. The country where the 1889 World's Fair was held.

   ☐ ☐ ☐ ☐ ◯ ☐

◯ ◯ ◯ ◯ ◯ ◯ ◯

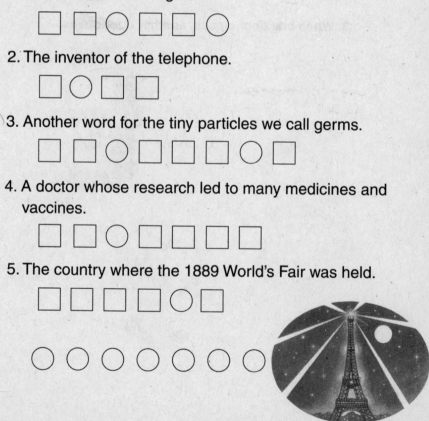

Answer key on page 245.

Secret Sayings

Match each magician's secret to the correct magician.

1. Chance favors the prepared mind.

**2. Genius is one percent inspiration and
    ninety-nine percent perspiration.**

3. When one door closes, another door opens.

a. Bell

b. Pasteur

c. Edison

Answer key on page 245.

Maze

Help Jack and Annie find a way to the top of the
Eiffel Tower before the evil sorcerer arrives!

Answer key on page 245.

Blizzard of the Blue Moon

Say Again?

Jack and Annie fight to save the unicorn Dianthus from Grinda and Balor. Draw in speech bubbles or thought bubbles and write in what Jack, Annie, Grinda, Balor, and Dianthus are saying or thinking at this point in the story.

Moon Message

Jack and Annie learn that a blue moon is when two full moons happen in the same month. Use the moon code below to find out what is one of Camelot's greatest treasures.

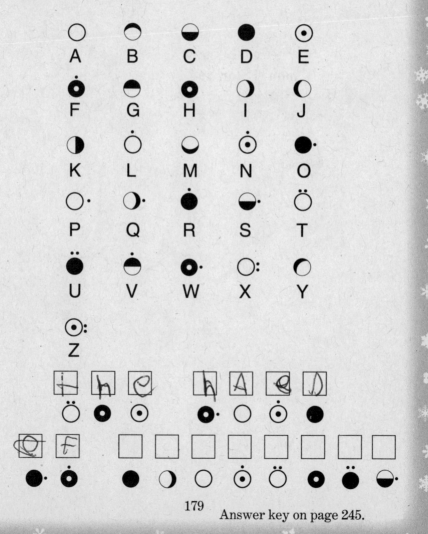

Answer key on page 245.

Different Dianthus

Jack and Annie save the unicorn Dianthus. Circle the Dianthus that is different from the rest.

Answer key on page 245.

Maze

Jack and Annie must find a unicorn in New York City, the largest city in the Western Hemisphere. Help them find their way out of Central Park and to the Cloisters.

Finish

Start

Answer key on page 245.

Illustrate It!

Tapestries were woven in the Middle Ages to tell stories. Draw a story on the tapestry below.

Dragon of the Red Dawn

Write Your Own Haiku!

As Jack and Annie found out in ancient Japan, anyone can be a poet! Haiku are simple but moving poems, often about nature or everyday life. Would you like to write your own? Get a pencil and give it a try!

Haiku are usually three lines long. Often the first line is five syllables long, the second line has seven syllables, and the third has five again. These are not strict rules, but they give an idea of how short a haiku really is.

Sit down and think about something you feel strongly about. It could be the beauty of the stars. It could be the comfort of a warm pair of mittens. Then write a simple three-line poem that makes people feel what you feel. That's your haiku!

_____

_____

_____

Passport Checklist

Jack and Annie do a lot of traveling! As they learn in Japan, most international travelers need a passport. Travelers collect stamps from each country they visit. You don't need a passport to travel within the United States, but it's fun to keep track of where you've been. Color in the states you have visited.

Alternative: Color in a state every time you see a car with a license plate from that state. You can make photocopies of this page and compete with friends and family on a road trip!

Rhyme Time

Teddy is using his magic ring and a rhyme to return to Camelot. But he's having trouble with his spells again! Choose the last line of the following spell to find the path to the correct castle. Only a proper rhyme will get Teddy home.

Tree house spins
And strong winds blow
Take me where

I've been before!

I want to go!

A myth come true!

Worth Quoting

The letters below are scrambled, but they are in the correct columns. Figure out where to place each letter to write out words of wisdom from Basho to Jack and Annie.

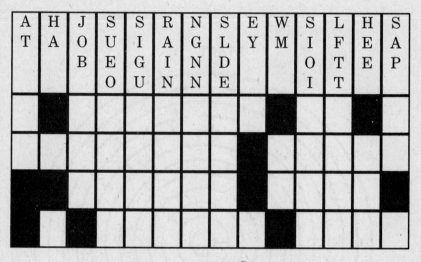

A	H	J	S	S	R	N	S	E	W	S	L	H	S
T	A	O	U	I	A	G	L	Y	M	I	F	E	A
		B	E	G	I	N	D			O	T	E	P
			O	U	N	N	E			I	T		

Answer key on page 245.

Maze

Jack and Annie are joining the firefighters of ancient Japan! Help them bring water from the river to the heart of the city before the fire spreads.

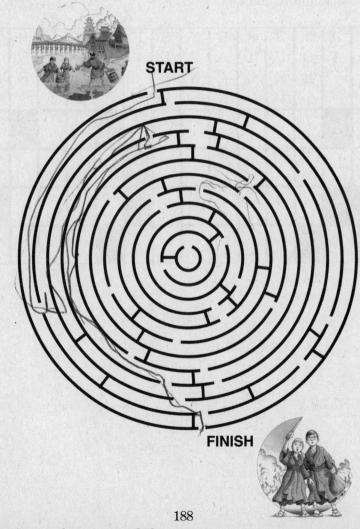

START

FINISH

Answer key on page 246.

Monday with a Mad Genius
Illustrate It!

In *Monday with a Mad Genius*, Jack and Annie use the Wand of Dianthus to grow bird wings. Imagine you could transform yourself in this way. Would you want duck feet for a day? The neck of a giraffe, or the tongue of a frog? Draw yourself in action with your new animal ability below.

Vocabulary Quiz

What common words today come from Latin? You might be surprised to realize how many Latin words are woven into the English language. Find words that include each of these prefixes. Write them in the boxes.

Example:

Bi- (two)

bicycle, bicentennial, billion, bifocal, biceps

Re- (again)	Cent- (one hundred)
Un- (not)	Flex- (to bend)
Auto- (self)	Dict- (to speak)

Answer key on page 246.

True and False

People throughout history have come up with many ideas to explain the world around them. Sometimes they have been right, but often they have been wrong. Even the brilliant Leonardo da Vinci had some ideas that seem very strange to us now. That's because we are always learning new facts about the world around us. Help Jack and Annie decide which of the following statements are true and which are false!

_____ The moon is made of cheese.

_____ Horses are descended from unicorns.

_____ Cows have many stomachs.

_____ The pyramids were built by space aliens.

_____ The Black Plague was spread by rats and fleas.

_____ Dinosaurs became extinct because humans polluted the earth.

_____ Birds can fly in part because they have hollow bones.

_____ Eating a lot of carrots can turn your skin orange.

_____ Plants grow toward sunlight.

_____ Tarantulas are deadly to human beings.

Answer key on page 246.

Code Breaker

Nightingales are known for their beautiful singing. Imagine that this nightingale is communicating with Annie using Morse code, which is an alphabet of simple sounds. Use the key below to decipher what the bird is saying.

Morse Code Alphabet Key

A .−	J .−−−	S ...
B −...	K −.−	T −
C −.−.	L .−..	U ..−
D −..	M −−	V ...−
E .	N −.	W .−−
F ..−.	O −−−	X −..−
G −−.	P .−−.	Y −.−−
H	Q −−.−	Z −−..
I ..	R .−.	

− .... −.− −. −.− −.−− −−− ..−
T   H   A   N   K   Y   O   U

..−. −−− .−. .−−. .−. . . .−.. .. −−.
F   O   R   F   R   E   E   I   N   G

−− . ..−. .−. −−− −− −− −.−−
M   E   F   R   O   M   M   Y

−.−. .− −−. .
C   A   G   E!

Answer key on page 246.

Code Maker

Leonardo da Vinci wrote his notes backward so they couldn't be read without a mirror. Choose a word and practice writing it like Leonardo.

Hint: Start practicing with the following letters. They will be the easiest to write backward.

A   W   T   Y   U   I
O   H   X   V   M

1. Write from right to left so the paper can be read from left to right. Have fun spelling words backward.

Example:

HOWDY _____

2. Write from right to left without changing the way you form your letters. Spell the words so the reader needs to read from right to left to understand your message.

Example:

YDWOH The letters do not change, just the order. _____

3. Write from right to left and flip the letters around so a mirror would be needed. This is easiest if you use a mirror while you write to check your work.

Example:

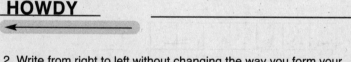 Flip the letters. _____

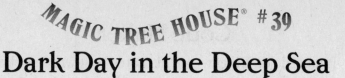

MAGIC TREE HOUSE® #39

Dark Day in the Deep Sea

Underwater Crisscross

Can you fill the puzzle with the names of all the animals pictured?

Answer key on page 246.

Seashell Riddle

The answer to the question below is hidden on a seashell. Start at the outside and work to the center of the shell. Write down all the letters on a white background. When you get to the center, go back in the other direction and write down the letters on a gray background.

How did Annie make enough money to buy a pet fish?

Answer key on page 246.

Matching

Using magic, Jack and Annie briefly gave an animal the ability to speak to humans. Imagine you could do the same thing with many different animals. Can you match the animal to what it might say? Choose wisely, because you can use each answer only once!

1. shark   **2. dolphin**   **3. koala**

4. bison   **5. monkey**

a. I'm cold-blooded. shark

b. I enjoy climbing trees. monkey

c. I'm warm-blooded. bison

d. I'm a fast swimmer. dolphin

e. I keep my babies in a pouch after they're born.

koala

Answer key on page 246.

Vocabulary Quiz

In *Dark Day in the Deep Sea*, Jack and Annie encounter a giant octopus. The prefix "oct-" always refers to eight of something. Use the word bank to aid you in labeling the drawings below.

> **Word Bank**
>
> Octagon   Octet   Octuplets
> Octave   Octopus

Octagon   _Octopus_   _Octet_

Octoplets   _Octave_

Answer key on page 247.

Science Challenge

A vertebrate is an animal with a backbone. Fish, amphibians, reptiles, birds, and mammals are all vertebrates.

An invertebrate is an animal without a backbone. Invertebrates include sponges, mollusks, and worms.

Only one of the following animals is an invertebrate. Can you figure out which one, using the information you've just learned?

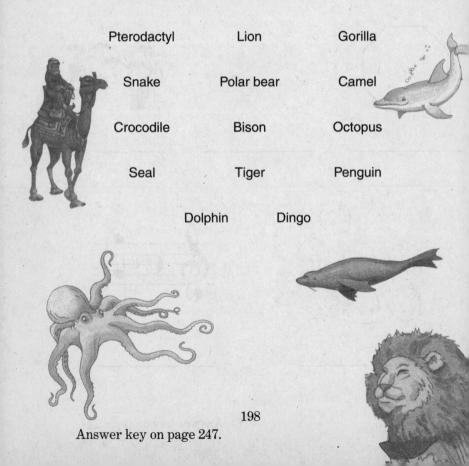

Pterodactyl Lion Gorilla

Snake Polar bear Camel

Crocodile Bison Octopus

Seal Tiger Penguin

Dolphin Dingo

Answer key on page 247.

Eve of the Emperor Penguin

Journalism Challenge

Jack and Annie found four secrets of happiness for Merlin. But most people have their own secrets to happiness. Ask several people in your life what they consider the most important secret to happiness. Then decide which secrets you agree with most strongly. Can you think of any of your own?

[Handwritten annotations: "dad", "family", "mom", "me", "love", "the love of family", "grandma"]

Logic Puzzle

Jack and Annie are writing a story about three penguins. Annie has given them names, and Jack has decided they will each be a different species of penguin. There will be one emperor penguin, one Galápagos penguin, and one little penguin. Each penguin lives either at the Equator, in Australia, or in Antarctica. And each penguin has ear feathers of a particular color—yellow, gray, or black.

Can you figure out which penguin is which? Use the grid to help you!

1. Lenny lives at the Equator.

2. Penny is not a Galápagos penguin.

3. The emperor penguin does not have black feathers around its ears.

4. Boo is a little penguin, and her ear feathers are not black or yellow.

5. The penguin that lives in Australia has gray ear feathers.

6. The emperor penguin lives in Antarctica.

Penguin	Location	Ear Color	Species
Lenny			
Penny			
Boo			

Answer key on page 247.

Code Breaker

Use the reverse alphabet code (A = Z, B = Y, C = X, and so on) to help Jack and Annie learn a surprising fact about penguins.

_____ _____

H L N V   K I V S R H G L I R X

_____ ____ __

K V M T F R M H   D V I V   Z H

____ __ _____.

G Z O O   Z H   K V L K O V

Answer key on page 247.

Science Challenge

Jack and Annie learned that people can get altitude sickness when they don't get enough oxygen. Oxygen is crucial to life on earth. But it also combines with other elements to form compounds in the air. A well-known example is carbon dioxide.

Carbon dioxide is formed when a carbon atom combines with two oxygen atoms. Its chemical formula is written CO_2, which means one carbon atom and two oxygen atoms. The prefix "di-" means "two."

If "O" stands for oxygen, "C" stands for carbon, and "N" stands for nitrogen, can you guess the chemical formula for nitrogen dioxide? Hint: "Nitrogen dioxide" sounds very similar to "carbon dioxide," doesn't it?

Answer: _____

Bonus: Can you guess the chemical formulas for these more difficult compounds? Use your knowledge of prefixes!

Dinitrogen trioxide: _____
Dinitrogen tetroxide: _____
Dinitrogen pentoxide: _____
Carbon monoxide: _____

202

Answer key on page 247.

Chart It!

In *Eve of the Emperor Penguin,* Nancy had three different jobs at the research station in Antarctica. When people live or work in groups, they have to share the work in order to get everything done. Although you don't live at a research station, you are part of a home. Let's take a look at some of the jobs done there.

What jobs are needed in your home?

Directions: Label each job with the person at home who normally takes care of the work.

Job	Person who does the job
Cook	_____
Clean	_____
Wash dishes	_____
Shop	_____
Remove trash	_____
Water plants	_____
Feed pets	_____
Drive	_____
Set tables for meals	_____

MAGIC TREE HOUSE® #41

Moonlight on the Magic Flute
Musical Notes

Wolfgang Amadeus Mozart was the most famous child musician in history. He left a message for Jack, Annie, and you in this piece of sheet music. A vertical line means a space between words.

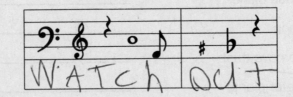

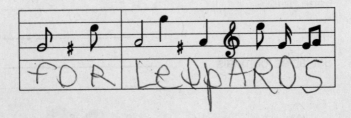

Answer key on page 247.

A Sound Study

How does Mozart's music compare to our music today? Play a recording of a piece of music by Mozart and then a piece of music from today. Fill in the Venn diagram below to compare and contrast the two pieces.

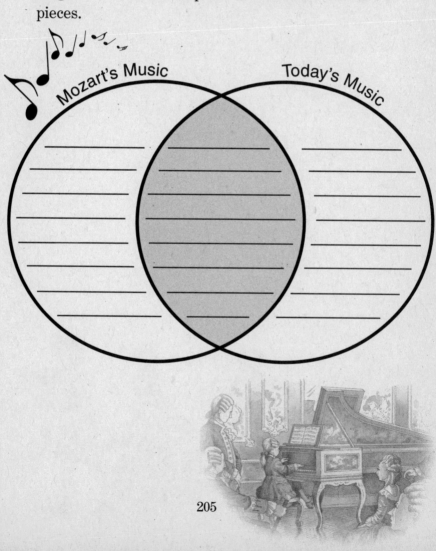

Mozart's Music

Today's Music

Illustrate It!

The summer palace of Empress Maria Theresa had one of the first zoos in the world. Draw the animals that are following Jack, Annie, and Wolfie.

Connect-the-Dots

Start at 1, and connect the dots to see what Jack is waving at.

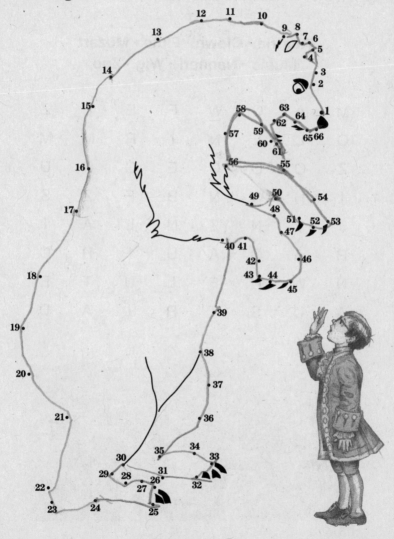

Answer key on page 247.

Word Search

Find and circle the words below. Words can go horizontally, vertically, or diagonally.

**Austria · Clown · Flute · Mozart
Music · Nannerl · Wig · Zoo**

```
M   A   C   W   F   E   L   Z
O   L   L   N   I   R   M   M
Z   O   Q   C   E   G   O   U
I   H   W   N   B   F   Z   S
J   V   N   Z   N   L   A   I
R   A   O   A   U   I   R   C
N   W   N   F   L   U   T   E
A   U   S   T   R   I   A   D
```

Answer key on page 248.

A Good Night for Ghosts

A Ghostly Survey

Little Mack, Happy, and Big Nose Sidney play a joke on Jack, Annie, and Dipper by pretending to be ghosts. But the ghosts get the last laugh when they really show up! Do you believe in ghosts? Conduct a survey by asking friends and family for their opinions about ghosts. Tally your results on the chart below.

Don't believe ghosts are real	Believe ghosts are real	Not sure
I|I		

How many people did you survey in total? 3

Write your results in fraction form on the chart below.		
Don't believe ghosts are real	Believe ghosts are real	Not sure
3	0	0

Spot the Differences

Jack and Annie meet the ghost of the pirate Jean Lafitte. Look at the picture on top. Then look at the picture on the bottom and circle the five differences.

Answer key on page 248.

Illustrate It!

November 1 is celebrated as All Saints' Day in New Orleans. Sometimes on the eve of All Saints' Day, people wear costumes and have parties and parades. What costume would you wear in the parade? Draw yourself celebrating the eve of All Saints' Day in New Orleans!

Musical Notes

Louis Armstrong grew up to be one of the greatest jazz musicians who ever lived. He left a message for Jack, Annie, and you in this piece of sheet music. A vertical line means a space between words.

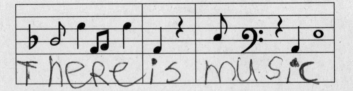

There is music

ALL Around you

Crossword Puzzle

Use the clues for Across and Down to fill in the puzzle spaces.

ACROSS

4. Famous pirate ghost
6. Oldest section of New Orleans
7. Louis Armstrong's nickname

DOWN

1. Instrument Louis Armstrong plays to entertain the ghosts
2. Music with a strong beat and played with lots of feeling
3. Train cars in the streets of New Orleans
5. What hardworking Dipper delivers

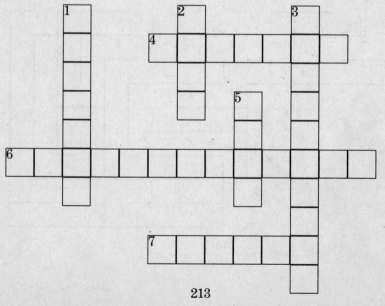

Answer key on page 248.

MAGIC TREE HOUSE® #43

Leprechaun in Late Winter

Maze

Help Jack and Annie follow Willy to the home of the Shee so they can rescue Augusta.

Finish

Start

Answer key on page 249.

Shee Scramble

The fairies of the Shee have a special message for Augusta—and you! Answer the questions and then unscramble the letters in the circles to discover the message.

1. Who wants to learn how to play the flute?

2. Where does Augusta live?

3. What is another word for "imaginative"?

4. Whom does Augusta want to see?

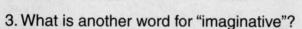

5. What is Willy?

Magic Tree House Time Line

In *Leprechaun in Late Winter,* Jack and Annie travel to Ireland in 1862. With the magic tree house, they have traveled to many different times and places. See if you can put these books in order by writing number 1 next to the book that takes place the farthest back in time and moving forward through history until you label number 6.

Answer key on page 249.

Match the Setting

Jack and Annie have been to Ireland before. Their first journey there took place during the Dark Ages. Draw a line from the cover of *Leprechaun in Late Winter* to the cover of the other Magic Tree House book set in Ireland.

Answer key on page 249.

What Are You Good At?

At the end of *Leprechaun in Late Winter*, Jack wonders what he's good for because he didn't know how to do anything on the Irish farm. Annie reminds him of all the things they've accomplished together. Below, write the things *you* are good at! Then decorate the page.

1. _____

2. _____

3. _____

4. _____

5. _____

MAGIC TREE HOUSE® #44

Choose the Next Adventure!

Where would you like Jack and Annie to go? Whom would you like them to help? Draw the next Magic Tree House cover below. Don't forget a title!

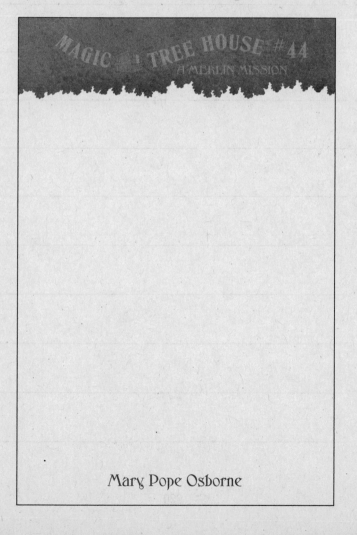

MAGIC TREE HOUSE® #44

A MERLIN MISSION

Mary Pope Osborne

Rank Your Favorite Books

Rank your favorite Magic Tree House books from #1–#5. Don't forget to say why!

1. _____

_____

2. _____

_____

3. _____

_____

4. _____

_____

5. _____

_____

Create a Cover

Create another Magic Tree House cover, but this time draw yourself as the main character in the adventure! Where would you like to go in the magic tree house? Don't forget a title!

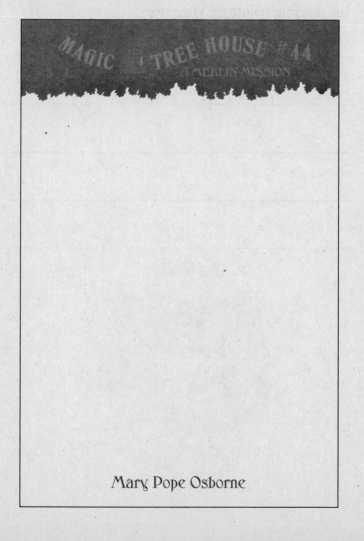

MAGIC TREE HOUSE #44
A MERLIN MISSION

Mary Pope Osborne

Research Book

Jack and Annie usually have the help of a research book on their adventures. Do some research about the place and time that you want to visit in the magic tree house. Take notes below, just like Jack! These can be the starting points for your story.

_____

_____

_____

_____

_____

Code Breaker

Congratulations on completing all of the Magic Tree House activities! Use the reverse alphabet code (A = Z, B = Y, C = X, and so on) to find out what Jack and Annie will be doing on their next mission.

_____
S V O K

_____   _____
X S Z I O V H   W R X P V M H

_____ __
D I R G V Z

_____
X S I R H G N Z H

_____.
G Z O V

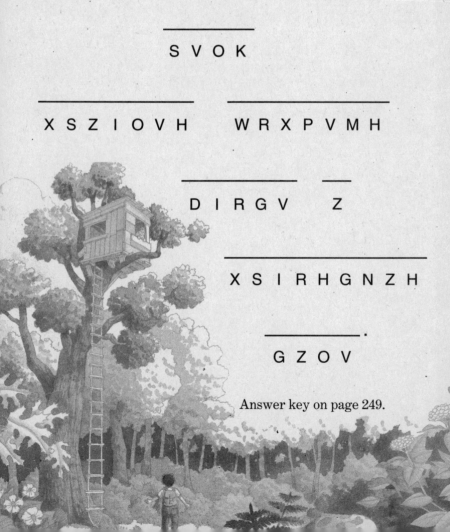

Answer key on page 249.

Answer Keys

page 1

page 2

page 4: Code Breaker

Answer: The wind begins to blow.

page 5

page 6

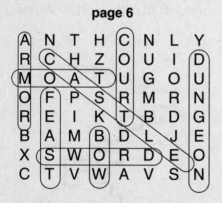

page 9: Matching

1. c 2. a 3. d 4. b

page 10

page 11

page 13: Code Breaker

Answer: Follow the cat to safety.

page 14: Mummy Scramble

Answers: Pyramid, Desert, Meow, Funeral, Ghost

Answer to circled letters: Wraps!

page 15

page 17

page 18

page 19

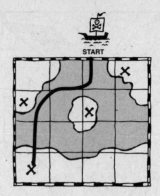

page 20: Code Breaker
Answer: The ship was on sail.

page 21: Ninja Note
Answer: Meet me in the cave.

page 23: Follow Nature
Answers: 1. b 2. e 3. c 4. f 5. a 6. d

page 25

page 26

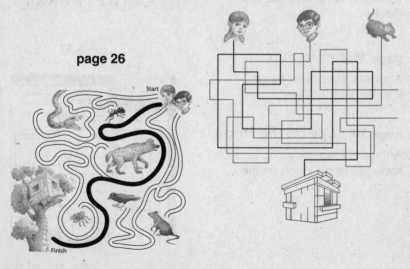

page 27

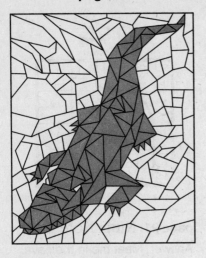

page 28: Matching

Answers: 1. c 2. d 3. b 4. a

page 30: Habitat Match

Answers: Jaguar, vampire bat, crocodile, monkey, butterfly, and army ant all belong in the Amazon rain forest.

page 31: Caveman Creations

Answers: 1. c 2. d 3. a 4. e 5. b

page 33

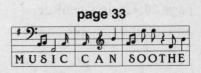

page 34: Cro-Magnon Wish List

Answers: Lightbulbs, Dinosaur soup, Eyeglasses, Books

page 35: Rebus Fun

Answers: Reindeer, Bison, Elk, Mammoth, Tiger

page 36: I Spy on the Moon

Answers: Flag, footprint, and rock can all be found on the moon.

page 37

page 38

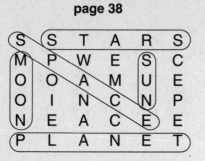

S	S	T	A	R	S	S
M	P	W	E			C
O	O	A	M	S	U	E
O	I	N	C	U	N	P
O	N	C	E		N	E
N	E	A	C	E		E
P	L	A	N	E	T	

Answer: We come in peace.

page 39

page 41

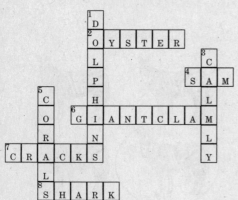

page 43

page 44

Finish

Start

page 46: Q & A Mix-up

Answers: What is a player piano? What are mustangs? Who were rustlers?

page 47: Ghost Town Scramble

Answers: Mustang, Horse, Saddle, Coffee, Canyon

Answer to circled letters: Soft hand

229

page 48

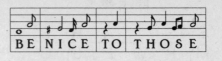

page 49

| BE | NICE | TO | THOSE |

| AROUND | YOU |

page 51: Morgan's Message

Answer: Be brave. Be wise. Be careful.

page 50

page 53

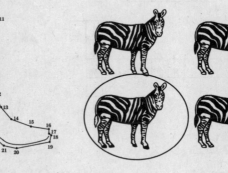

page 54

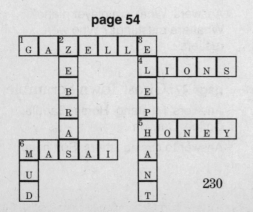

230

page 55: Rebus Fun

Answers: Lion, Hippopotamus, Morgan le Fay, Monkey, Annie

page 56: Polar Bear Sci

Answers: 1. Mask 2. Seal Hu 3. Dogsled 4. Northern Lights

Answer to circled letters: Home

page 57

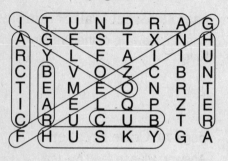

page 58

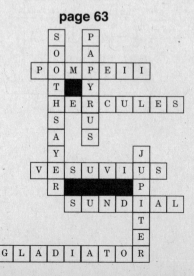

page 60

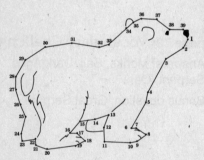

page 61: Matching

Answers: 1. Jupiter 2. Neptune 3. Minerva 4. Venus 5. Mars 6. Cupid 7. Mercury 8. Diana 9. Saturn 10. Ceres

page 62: Vocabulary Challenge

Possible answers: Flexible, legend, pedal, depend, portable, scribble, sense, spectator, victory, vocal

page 63

231

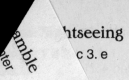

page 65: Worth Quoting

Answer: When in Rome do as the Romans do.

e 67

page 69

page 68: Great Wall Scramble

Answer: Beware of the Dragon King.

page 70: Code Breaker

Answer: Please feed me tea leaves.

page 72: Vocabulary Challenge

Answers: Monks, Sail, Dark Ages, Serpent, Oars

Bonus question: Great Serpent

page 73: Writers Across the Ages

Answers: 1. a 2. c 3. b

Bonus question: A computer

page 74

page 76

page 77

page 78: Vocabulary Challenge

Answers: 1. d 2. c 3. e 4. a 5. b

page 79

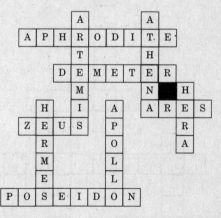

page 80: Code Breaker

Answers:
Jack is smart.
Pegasus is pretty.
Morgan is kind.

page 81

page 83

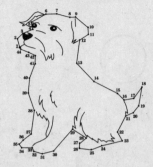

page 82: Code Breaker

Answer: Watch out for icebergs.

page 85: Compass Game

Answer: N 1 block, NW 1 block, W 1 block, N 2 blocks, E 1 block, N 1 block.

page 84

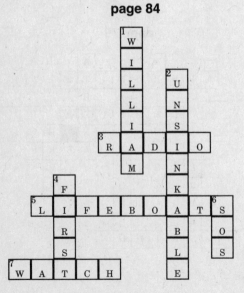

page 86

page 89: Waste Not, Want Not

Answers: 1. c 2. f 3. a 4. e 5. d 6. b

234

page 90

page 91

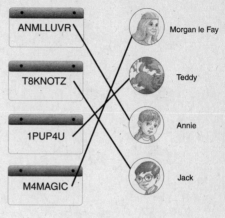

ANMLLUVR

T8KNOTZ

1PUP4U

M4MAGIC

Morgan le Fay

Teddy

Annie

Jack

page 93

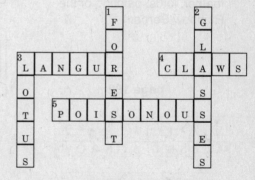

page 92: Peacock Puzzle

Answer: Greedy poachers are hunting tigers.

page 94: Python Puzzle

Answer: Crush.

page 96: Habitat Match

Answers: 1. America 2. Australia
3. India 4. America 5. Australia
6. Australia 7. India 8. Australia
9. India 10. India

page 97

page 99

page 100: Break the Spell!

Answers: Pocket watch, feather, lotus, painting of the Rainbow Serpent

page 101

page 102

LESSEN SORROW

AND GIVE HOPE

page 103

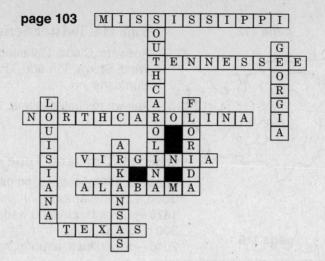

page 104

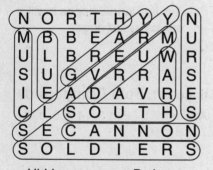

Hidden message: Be brave.

page 108: Code Breaker

Answer: The British are coming!

page 109

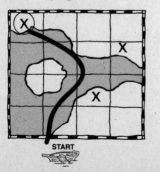

page 110: Matching

Answers: 1. b 2. d 3. l 4. e
5. a 6. g 7. f 8. c 9. m 10. h
11. i 12. k 13. j

237

page 112

page 114: Twister Scramble

Answers: Cloud, Lightning, Wind, Storm, Tornado, Thunder, Hurricane

Answer to circled letters: Climate

page 115: Time and Time Again

Answers: **1800**—tepees, 40 million bison, Lakota warriors.
1870—railroads, covered wagons, 300 bison, dugouts.
2010—power lines, airports, hospitals.

page 116

Family	Wagon Size	Home State	Pet
Osbornes	large	Connecticut	dog
Washingtons	medium	Virginia	bird
Bartons	small	New York	cat

page 117: Vortex Riddle

Answer: Annie hopes it will rain cats and dogs.

page 121: Split Compounds

Answers: 1. f 2. h 3. i 4. d 5. e 6. b 7. g 8. c 9. a

page 122

238

page 123

page 128

Finish

Start

page 126

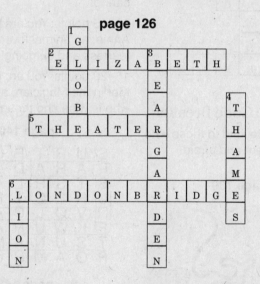

page 129

page 131: Sign Language Code
Answer: Protect the gentle giants.

239

page 132: Gorilla Diet Scramble

Answers: Leaves, Twigs, Flowers, Bamboo

Answer to circled letters: Meat

page 135

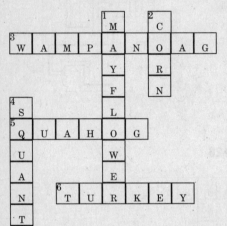

page 136: Code Breaker

Answer: Be kind to those who feel different and afraid.

page 139

page 134: Which Magic Tree House Character Are You?

Question 1: a = 1 pt. b = 3 pts. c = 5 pts.

Question 2: a = 3 pts. b = 1 pt. c = 5 pts.

Question 3: a = 5 pts. b = 3 pts. c = 1 pt.

Question 4: a = 1 pt. b = 5 pts. c = 3 pts.

4–9 points: You are like Jack, a cautious kid who is smart and caring!

10–15 points: You are like Annie, an animal lover who is fearless and outgoing!

16–20 points: You are like Merlin the Magician, a leader who is wise and thoughtful!

page 140

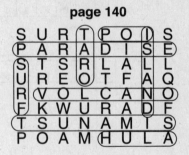

page 142

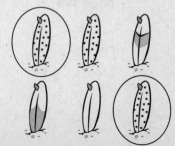

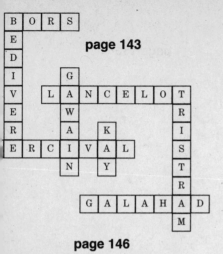

page 143

page 144

G A M A I C I M
C I A M G M A G
A M G I A I C M
C A I A M G I G
I G M C M A I A
G C G A M G M C
A M G I C A A M
C I M C I M G A

page 147: Rhyme Time
Answers: silk, syrup, team

page 146

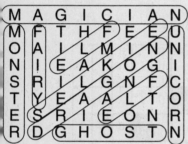

M A G I C I A N
M F T H F E E U
O A I L M I N N
N I E A K O G I
S R I L G N F C
T Y E A A L T O
E S R I E O N R
R D G H O S T N

Answer: The imagination

page 150: Code Breaker
Answer: They should just wing it.

page 151: Optical Illusion
Answer: Boo!

page 152: Math Puzzle

Morgan gets 10 pieces.

Merlin gets 2 pieces.

Teddy gets 4 pieces.

Kathleen gets 4 pieces.

page 149

Kid	Costume	Carrying	Color
Jack	spider	pumpkin	purple
Annie	bird	pillowcase	black
Teddy	dog	basket	brown

page 153

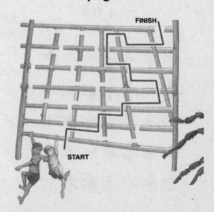

241

page 154: Shell Scramble

Answer: Choose peace and lose war.

page 155: Rhyme Time

Possible answers: Over there!
And flame burn bright!
A bumblebee!

page 156

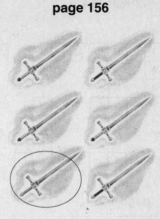

page 158

W	H	E	N	F	T	O	S	S	A	G	A	B	S	H
I	I	N	T	F	T		S	S		G	A	B	S	H
T	H	S		O	R		I	E		H	I	A	U	T
I	S		N	E	R		R	T		L		R	N	T
T	H	E	■	F	R	O	S	T	■	G	I	A	N	T
I	S	■	N	O	T	■	R	E	A	L	■	B	U	T
W	I	N	T	E	R	■	I	S	■	H	A	R	S	H

page 159

page 160: Winter Scramble

Answer: Snow, Hail, Cold, Cloud, Sleet, Blizzard, Ice, Frost

Answer to circled letters: Shoulder

page 161

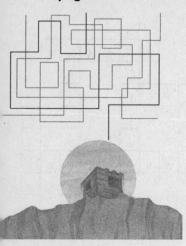

page 164

page 165

page 166

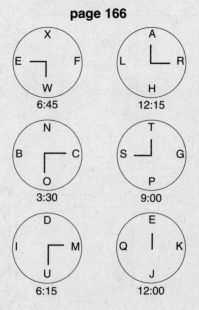

X
E   F
W
6:45

A
L   R
H
12:15

N
B   C
O
3:30

T
S   G
P
9:00

D
I   M
U
6:15

E
Q   K
J
12:00

Wear Costume

page 167

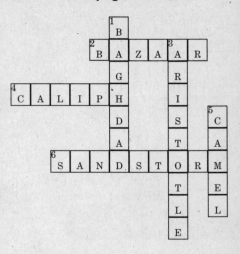

page 168

```
        1
        B
    2       3
    B A Z A R A R
        A   R
    4       G   I
    C A L I P H S   5
        D   T   C
        A   T   A
    6           M
    S A N D S T O R M E
        T   L   L
        E   E
```

page 169

page 170: Mystic Math

$12 - 4 = 8$ (h) $9 + 9 = 18$ (r)

$2 + 3 = 5$ (e) $7 - 6 = 1$ (a)

$15 - 11 = 4$ (d) $5 + 14 = 19$ (s)

Answer: Shared

page 173

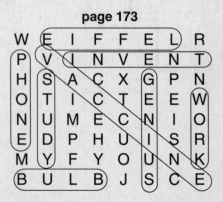

page 175: Scrambled Scientists

Answers: 1. Edison 2. Bell
3. Microbes 4. Pasteur 5. France

Answer to circled letters: Science

page 176: Secret Sayings

Answers: 1. b 2. c 3. a

page 180

page 177

page 181

page 179: Moon Message

Answer: The wand of Dianthus

page 186: Rhyme Time

Answer: I want to go!

page 187

A	H	J	S	S	R	N	S	E	W	S	L	H	S
T	A	J	U	I	A	G	L	Y	M	I	F	E	A
		O	E	G	I	N	D		M	O	T	E	P
		B	O	U	N	N	E			I	T		
A		J	O	U	R	N	E	Y		O	F		A
T	H	O	U	S	A	N	D		M	I	L	E	S
		B	E	G	I	N	S		W	I	T	H	
	A		S	I	N	G	L	E		S	T	E	P

page 188

START

FINISH

page 190: Vocabulary Quiz

Possible answers: return, redo; century, centennial; unclear, undo; flexible, flexing; automobile, automatic; dictate, dictionary

page 191: True and False

Answers: F, F, T, F, T, F, T, T, T, F

page 192: Code Breaker

Answer: Thank you for freeing me from my cage!

page 194

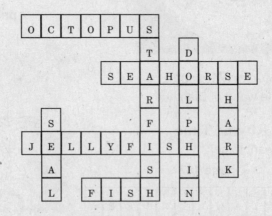

page 195: Seashell Riddle

Answer: She sold seashells by the seashore.

page 196: Matching

Answers: 1. a 2. d 3. e 4. c 5. b

page 197: Vocabulary Quiz

Answers: Octagon, Octopus, Octet, Octuplets, Octave

page 198: Science Challenge

Answer: Octopus

page 200

Penguin	Location	Ear Color	Species
Lenny	Equator	black	Galápagos
Penny	Antarctica	yellow	emperor
Boo	Australia	gray	little

page 201: Code Breaker

Answer: Some prehistoric penguins were as tall as people.

page 202: Science Challenge

Answer: NO_2

Bonus: N_2O_3, N_2O_4, N_2O_5, CO

page 204

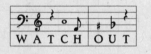

WATCH OUT

FOR LEOPARDS

page 207

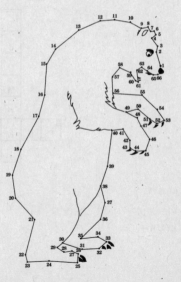

page 208

M	A	C	W	F	E	L	Z
O	L	L	N	I	R	M	M
Z	O	O	C	E	G	O	U
I	H	W	N	B	F	Z	S
J	V	N	Z	N	L	A	I
R	A	O	A	U	I	R	C
N	W	N	F	L	U	T	E
A	U	S	T	R	I	A	D

page 210

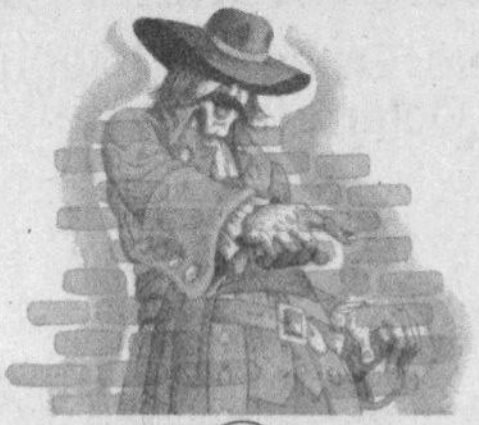

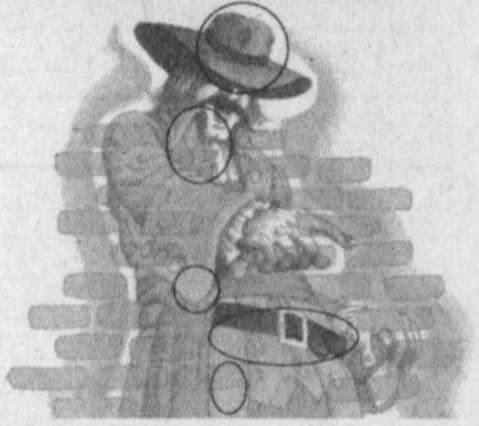

page 212

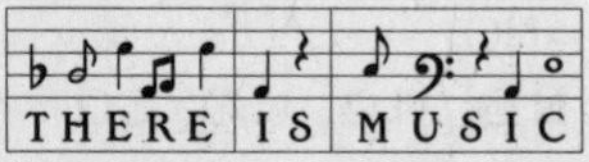
THERE IS MUSIC

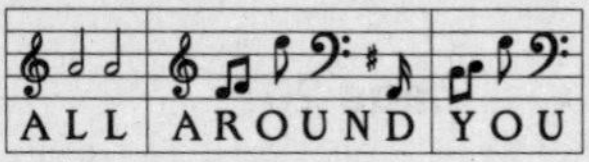
ALL AROUND YOU

page 213

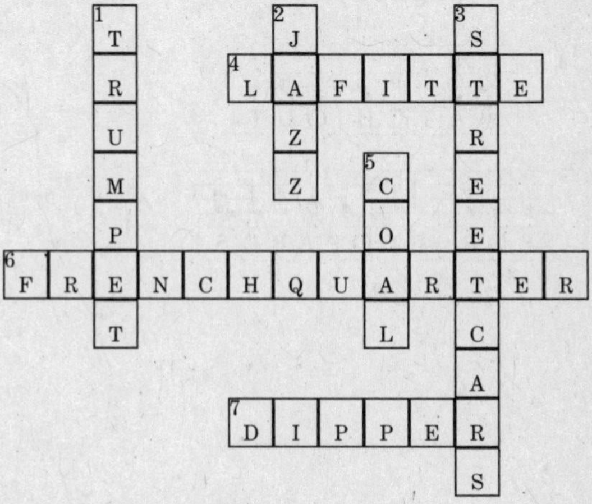
1 TRUMPET
2 JAZZ
3 STREETCARS
4 LAFITTE
5 COAL
6 FRENCHQUARTER
7 DIPPER

page 214

page 215: Shee Scramble
Answers: 1. Willy 2. Big House
3. Creative 4. Shee 5. Leprechaun
Answer to circled letters: Believe!

page 216: Magic Tree House Time Line

1. *Sunset of the Sabertooth*
2. *Hour of the Olympics*
3. *Season of the Sandstorms*
4. *Stage Fright on a Summer Night*
5. *Revolutionary War on Wednesday*
6. *Civil War on Sunday*

page 217: Match the Setting
Answer: *Viking Ships at Sunrise*

page 223: Code Breaker
Answer: Help Charles Dickens write a Christmas tale.

CAPQATE

BET

bɘoWL

VARₛoɛɬ

GOOd GOB

GOOd GOB

RHCB

Guess what?

Jack and Annie have a musical CD!

For more information about
MAGIC TREE HOUSE: THE MUSICAL
(including how to order the CD!),
visit www.mthmusical.com.